Biblical Quotes
For Life

Dr. Robert Osobase

Biblical Quotes For Life

Published by Cornerstone Publishing

A Division of Cornerstone Creativity Group LLC
Info@thecornerstonepublishers.com
www.thecornerstonepublishers.com

Author's Contact

To book the author to speak at your next event or to order bulk copies of this book, please, use the information below:

rovic72@gmail.com

Printed in the United States of America.

Dedication

To the honor of the Almighty God, and to my Savior, Jesus Christ, whose steadfast love and limitless grace have led me through life's highs and lows. May this book glorify your name and ignite souls to pursue your everlasting light.

Contents

Introduction

Welcome to "Biblical Quotes for Life," a compilation that delves into the timeless wisdom and guidance found in the pages of the Bible. This book is a treasure trove of inspiration, offering profound insights into various facets of life, relationships, spirituality, and personal development. The Bible, with its rich tapestry of verses, serves as a source of solace, strength, and enlightenment for people from all walks of life.

As we embark on this journey through biblical quotes, we will explore the transformative power of divine words across a spectrum of essential themes. Each chapter is meticulously crafted to provide insight and guidance for navigating the complexities of life, drawing upon the wisdom encapsulated in the scriptures.

May you find inspiration, guidance, and a deeper connection with the eternal truths that have withstood the test of time. May these verses resonate in your heart and illuminate your journey towards a life rooted in faith, love, and wisdom.

1

QUOTES FOR EDUCATION AND WISDOM

This chapter's compilation serves as a timeless reservoir of education and wisdom, providing a foundation for ethical living, personal growth, and spiritual reflection. Discover the profound teachings and insights that the Bible imparts on education and the pursuit of wisdom. These verses inspire a lifelong quest for knowledge and understanding.

1. **Proverbs 1:7** - *"The fear of the Lord is the beginning of knowledge, but fools despise wisdom and instruction."*

2. **Proverbs 4:5** - *"Get wisdom, get understanding; do not forget my words or turn away from them."*

3. **Proverbs 16:21** - *"The wise in heart are called discerning, and gracious words promote instruction."*

4. **Psalm 119:66** - *"Teach me knowledge and good judgment, for I trust your commands."*

5. **Proverbs 12:15** - *"The way of a fool is right in his own eyes, but a wise man listens to advice."*

6. **Proverbs 14:27** - *"The fear of the Lord is a fountain of life, turning a person from the snares of death."*

7. **Proverbs 23:15** - *"My son, if your heart is wise, then my heart will be glad indeed."*

8. **Proverbs 2:6** - *"For the Lord gives wisdom; from his mouth comes knowledge and understanding."*

9. **Proverbs 9:9** - *"Instruct the wise and they will be wiser still; teach the righteous and they will add to their learning."*

10. **Proverbs 16:23** - *"A wise man's heart guides his mouth, and his lips promote instruction."*

11. **Proverbs 3:35** - *"The wise will inherit honor, but fools get disgrace."*

12. **Proverbs 19:20** - *"Listen to advice and accept discipline, and at the end, you will be counted among the wise."*

13. **Proverbs 9:10** - *"The fear of the Lord is the beginning of wisdom, and knowledge of the Holy One is understanding."*

14. **Proverbs 23:12** - *"Apply your heart to instruction and your ears to words of knowledge."*

15. **Hosea 4:6** - *"My people are destroyed for lack of knowledge; because you have rejected knowledge, I reject you from being a priest to me."*

16. **Proverbs 13:20** - *"Whoever walks with the wise becomes wise, but the companion of fools will suffer harm."*

17. **Proverbs 18:15** - *"An intelligent heart acquires knowledge, and the ear of the wise seeks knowledge."*

18. **Proverbs 15:14** - *"The heart of the discerning acquires knowledge, for the ears of the wise seek it out."*

19. **Proverbs 16:21** - *"The wisdom of heart is called discerning, and sweetness of speech increases persuasiveness."*

20. **Proverbs 1:5** - *"Let the wise hear and increase in learning, and the one who understands obtain guidance."*

21. **Proverbs 8:11** - *"For wisdom is better than jewels, and all that you may desire cannot compare with her."*

22. **Proverbs 18:2** - *"A fool takes no pleasure in understanding, but only in expressing his opinion."*

23. **Proverbs 9:9** - *"Give instruction to a wise man, and he will be still wiser; teach a righteous man, and he will increase in learning."*

24. **Psalm 119:13** - *"The unfolding of your words gives light; it imparts understanding to the simple."*

25. **Proverbs 19:8** - *"Whoever gets sense loves his own soul; he who keeps understanding will discover good."*

26. **Romans 12:2** - *"Do not be conformed to this world, but be transformed by the renewal of your mind, that by testing you may discern what is the will of God, what is good and acceptable and perfect."*

27. **Jeremiah 29:11** - *"For I know the plans I have for you, declares the Lord, plans for welfare and not for evil, to give you a future and a hope."*

28. **Proverbs 3:5** - *"Trust in the Lord with all your heart, and do not lean on your own understanding."*

29. **Proverbs 3:13** - *"Blessed is the one who finds wisdom, and the one who gets understanding."*

30. **Psalm 19:7** - *"The law of the Lord is perfect, reviving the soul; the testimony of the Lord is sure, making wise the simple."*

31. **Proverbs 15:3** - *"The eyes of the Lord are in every place, keeping watch on the evil and the good."*

32. **Proverbs 15:28** - *"The heart of the righteous ponders how to answer, but the mouth of the wicked pours out evil things."*

33. **Proverbs 14:27** - *"The fear of the Lord is a fountain of life, turning people away from the snares of death."*

34. **Proverbs 3:1** - *"My son, do not forget my teaching, but let your heart keep my commandments."*

35. **Proverbs 15:5** - *"A fool despises his father's instruction, but whoever heeds reproof is prudent."*

36. **James 3:17** - *"But the wisdom from above is first pure, then peaceable, gentle, open to reason, full of mercy and good fruits, impartial and sincere."*

37. **Psalm 111:10** - *"The fear of the Lord is the beginning of wisdom; all those who practice it have a good understanding. His praise endures forever!"*

38. **James 1:5** - *"If any of you lacks wisdom, let him ask God, who gives generously to all without reproach, and it will be given him."*

39. **Proverbs 3:3** - *"Let not steadfast love and faithfulness forsake you; bind them around your neck; write them on the tablet of your heart."*

40. **John 14:26** - *"But the Helper, the Holy Spirit, whom the Father will send in my name, he will teach you all things and bring to your remembrance all that I have said to you."*

41. **Hosea 4:6** - *"My people are destroyed for lack of knowledge; because you have rejected knowledge, I reject you from being a priest to me. And since you have forgotten the law of your God, I also will forget your children."*

42. **Proverbs 16:20** - *"Whoever gives thought to the word will discover good, and blessed is he who trusts in the Lord."*

43. **Proverbs 23:23** - *"Buy the truth and do not sell it— wisdom, instruction, and insight as well."*

44. **Proverbs 4:7** - *"The beginning of wisdom is this: Get wisdom. Though it cost all you have, get understanding."*

45. **Proverbs 2:6** - *"The Lord gives wisdom; from his mouth comes knowledge and understanding."*

46. **Proverbs 2:10** - *"For wisdom will enter your heart, and knowledge will be pleasant to your soul."*

47. **Proverbs 15:28** - *"The heart of the righteous weighs its answers, but the mouth of the wicked gushes evil."*

48. **Proverbs 12:15** - *"The way of fools seems right to them, but the wise listen to advice."*

49. **Proverbs 27:17** - *"As iron sharpens iron, so one person sharpens another."*

50. **Proverbs 14:16** - *"A wise man fears the Lord and shuns evil, but a fool is hotheaded and yet feels secure."*

51. **Proverbs 10:8** - *"The wise in heart accept commands, but a chattering fool comes to ruin."*

52. **Proverbs 12:25** - *"Anxiety weighs down the heart, but a kind word cheers it up."*

53. **Proverbs 8:13** - *"To fear the Lord is to hate evil; I hate pride and arrogance, evil behavior and perverse speech."*

54. **Proverbs 3:7** - *"Do not be wise in your own eyes; fear the Lord and shun evil."*

55. **Proverbs 10:1** - *"A wise son brings joy to his father, but a foolish son brings grief to his mother."*

56. **Proverbs 9:9** - *"Instruct the wise and they will be wiser still; teach the righteous and they will add to their learning."*

57. **Proverbs 24:5** - *"A wise man is full of strength, and a man of knowledge enhances his might."*

58. **Proverbs 4:6** - *"Do not forsake wisdom, and she will protect you; love her, and she will watch over you."*

59. **Proverbs 13:1** - *"A wise man listens to advice, but a mocker does not respond to rebukes."*

60. **Proverbs 29:11** - *"A fool gives full vent to his anger, but a wise man keeps himself under control."*

61. **Proverbs 10:13** - *"Wisdom is found on the lips of the discerning, but a rod is for the back of one who has no sense."*

62. **Proverbs 12:15** - *"The way of the fool is right in his own eyes, but a wise man listens to advice."*

63. **Proverbs 19:23** - *"The fear of the Lord leads to life, and whoever has it rests satisfied; he will not be visited by harm."*

64. **Proverbs 10:1** - *"A wise son makes a glad father, but a foolish son is a sorrow to his mother."*

65. **Psalm 23:1-3** - *"The Lord is my shepherd; I shall not want. He makes me lie down in green pastures. He leads me beside still waters. He restores my soul. He leads me in paths of righteousness for his name's sake."*

66. **Proverbs 10:14** - *"The wise lay up knowledge, but the mouth of a fool brings ruin near."*

67. **Proverbs 15:33** - *"The fear of the Lord is instruction in wisdom, and humility comes before honor."*

68. **Psalm 145:18** - *"The Lord is near to all who call on him, to all who call on him in truth."*

69. **Proverbs 13:1** - *"A wise son hears his father's instruction, but a scoffer does not listen to rebuke."*

70. **Proverbs 3:35** - *"The wise will inherit honor, but fools get disgrace."*

71. **Proverbs 15:20** - *"A wise son makes a glad father, but a foolish man despises his mother."*

72. **Proverbs 1:8** - *"Hear, my son, your father's instruction, and forsake not your mother's teaching."*

73. **Proverbs 15:20** - *"A wise son makes a glad father, but a foolish man despises his mother."*

74. **Proverbs 3:35** - *"The wise will inherit honor, but fools get disgrace."*

75. **Proverbs 13:20** - *"He who walks with the wise grows wise, but a companion of fools suffers harm."*

2

LOVE OF GOD
AND MAN

This chapter explores the profound themes of love depicted in the Bible. It delves into timeless verses that depict the boundless love of God for humanity and inspire compassion and empathy among individuals. Through poignant quotes and reflections, the chapter invites readers to explore the transformative nature of love in both our relationship with the divine and our interactions with one another.

1. **John 3:16:** - *"For God so loved the world, that he gave his only Son, that whoever believes in him should not perish but have eternal life."*

2. **John 13:34:** - *"A new command I give you: Love one another. As I have loved you, so you must love one another."*

3. **1 John 4:7:** - *"Beloved, let us love one another, for love is from God, and whoever loves has been born of God and knows God."*

4. **Romans 5:8:** - *"But God shows his love for us in that while we were still sinners, Christ died for us."*

5. **1 Corinthians 13:13:** - *"And now these three remain: faith, hope, and love. But the greatest of these is love."*

6. **1 John 4:19:** - *"We love because he first loved us."*

7. **1 Corinthians 16:14:** - *"Let all that you do be done in love."*

8. **Romans 13:8:** - *"Owe no one anything, except to love each other, for the one who loves another has fulfilled the law."*

9. **1 Peter 4:8:** - *"Above all, keep loving one another earnestly, since love covers a multitude of sins."*

10. **1 Corinthians 13:4:** - *"Love is patient, love is kind. It does not envy, it does not boast, it is not proud."*

11. **1 Corinthians 16:14:** - *"Do everything in love."*

12. **Romans 12:9:** - *"Let love be genuine. Abhor what is evil; hold fast to what is good."*

13. **Colossians 3:14:** - *"And above all these put on love, which binds everything together in perfect harmony."*

14. **Luke 6:35:** - *"But love your enemies, and do good, and lend, expecting nothing in return, and your reward will be great, and you will be sons of the Most High, for he is kind to the ungrateful and the evil."*

15. **1 John 4:10:** - *"In this is love, not that we have loved God but that he loved us and sent his Son to be the propitiation for our sins."*

16. **Zephaniah 3:17:** - *"The Lord your God is in your midst, a mighty one who will save; he will rejoice over you with gladness; he will quiet you by his love; he will exult over you with loud singing."*

17. **John 15:13:** - *"Greater love has no one than this, that someone lay down his life for his friends."*

18. **Psalm 143:8:** - *"Let the morning bring me word of your unfailing love, for I have put my trust in you. Show me the way I should go, for to you I entrust my life."*

19. **Galatians 2:20:** - *"I have been crucified with Christ. It is no longer I who live, but Christ who lives in me. And the life I now live in the flesh I live by faith in the Son of God, who loved me and gave himself for me."*

20. **Lamentations 3:22-23:** - *"The steadfast love of the Lord never ceases; his mercies never come to an end; they are new every morning; great is your faithfulness."*

21. **Psalm 86:15:** - *"But you, O Lord, are a God merciful and gracious, slow to anger and abounding in steadfast love and faithfulness."*

22. **1 John 3:1:** - *"See what kind of love the Father has given to us, that we should be called children of God; and so we are. The reason why the world does not know us is that it did not know him."*

23. **Psalm 116:1:** - *"I love the Lord, because he has heard my voice and my pleas for mercy."*

24. **Romans 8:37:** - *"No, in all these things we are more than conquerors through him who loved us."*

25. **Romans 5:5:** - *"And hope does not put us to shame, because God's love has been poured into our hearts through the Holy Spirit who has been given to us."*

26. **Psalm 86:15:** - *"But you, O Lord, are a God merciful and gracious, slow to anger and abounding in steadfast love and faithfulness."*

27. **John 13:35:** - *"By this all people will know that you are my disciples if you have love for one another."*

28. **2 Thessalonians 3:5:** - *"May the Lord direct your hearts into the love of God and into the steadfastness of Christ."*

29. **Nahum 1:7:** - *"The Lord is good, a stronghold in the day of trouble; he knows those who take refuge in him."*

30. **1 John 4:8:** - *"Whoever does not love does not know God, because God is love."*

31. **Ephesians 2:4-5:** - *"But God, being rich in mercy, because of the great love with which he loved us, even when we were dead in our trespasses, made us alive together with Christ—by grace you have been saved."*

32. **2 Corinthians 5:14:** - *"The love of Christ compels us."*

33. **John 15:9:** - *"As the Father has loved me, so have I loved you. Abide in my love."*

34. **1 Thessalonians 3:12:** - *"May the Lord make your love increase and overflow for each other and for everyone else, just as ours does for you."*

35. **Ephesians 5:2:** - *"And walk in love, as Christ loved us and gave himself up for us, a fragrant offering and sacrifice to God."*

36. **Psalm 86:15:** - *"But you, O Lord, are a God merciful and gracious, slow to anger and abounding in steadfast love and faithfulness."*

37. **Galatians 5:22:** - *"But the fruit of the Spirit is love, joy, peace, forbearance, kindness, goodness, faithfulness."*

38. **Romans 12:10:** - *"Love one another with brotherly affection. Outdo one another in showing honor."*

39. **1 John 4:19:** - *"We love because he first loved us."*

40. **1 John 4:16:** - *"So we have come to know and to believe the love that God has for us. God is love, and anyone who abides in love abides in God, and God abides in them."*

41. **Ephesians 4:2:** - *"With all humility and gentleness, with patience, bearing with one another in love."*

42. **Luke 6:35:** - *"But love your enemies, and do good, and lend, expecting nothing in return, and your reward will be great, and you will be sons of the Most High, for he is kind to the ungrateful and the evil."*

43. **Psalm 103:8:** - *"The Lord is merciful and gracious, slow to anger and abounding in steadfast love."*

44. **Proverbs 3:3:** - *"Let not steadfast love and faithfulness forsake you; bind them around your neck; write them on the tablet of your heart."*

45. **Colossians 3:14:** - *"And above all these put on love, which binds everything together in perfect harmony."*

46. **Mark 12:31:** - *"Love your neighbor as yourself."*

47. **Zephaniah 3:17:** - *"The Lord your God is in your midst, a mighty one who will save; he will rejoice over you with gladness; he will quiet you by his love; he will exult over you with loud singing."*

48. **Romans 12:9:** - *"Let love be genuine. Abhor what is evil; hold fast to what is good."*

49. **Ephesians 5:25:** - *"Husbands, love your wives, as Christ loved the church and gave himself up for her."*

50. **Proverbs 10:12:** - *"Hatred stirs up strife, but love covers all offenses."*

51. **1 Peter 4:8:** - *"Above all, keep loving one another earnestly, since love covers a multitude of sins."*

52. **1 John 4:11:** - *"Beloved, if God so loved us, we also ought to love one another."*

53. **Romans 12:9:** - *"Let love be without hypocrisy. Abhor what is evil; cling to what is good."*

54. **1 Corinthians 13:13:** - *"And now these three remain: faith, hope, and love. But the greatest of these is love."*

55. **Psalm 86:15:** - *"But you, O Lord, are a God merciful and gracious, slow to anger and abounding in steadfast love and faithfulness."*

56. **Galatians 5:22:** - *"But the fruit of the Spirit is love, joy, peace, forbearance, kindness, goodness, faithfulness."*

57. **1 John 4:8:** - *"Anyone who does not love does not know God, because God is love."*

58. **Proverbs 17:17:** - *"A friend loves at all times, and a brother is born for adversity."*

59. **1 John 4:16:** - *"And we have known and believed the love that God has for us. God is love, and he who abides in love abides in God, and God in him."*

60. **1 Corinthians 13:13:** - *"So now faith, hope, and love abide, these three; but the greatest of these is love."*

61. **Luke 6:35:** - *"But love your enemies, and do good, and lend, expecting nothing in return, and your reward will be great, and you will be sons of the Most High, for he is kind to the ungrateful and the evil."*

62. **1 John 4:18:** - *"There is no fear in love, but perfect love casts out fear. For fear has to do with punishment, and whoever fears has not been perfected in love."*

63. **John 13:34:** - *"A new command I give you: Love one another. As I have loved you, so you must love one another."*

64. **John 15:12:** - *"This is my commandment, that you love one another as I have loved you."*

65. **John 15:9:** - *"As the Father has loved me, so have I loved you. Abide in my love."*

66. **Ephesians 2:4:** - *"But God, being rich in mercy, because of the great love with which he loved us."*

67. **Psalm 86:15:** - *"But you, O Lord, are a God merciful and gracious, slow to anger and abounding in steadfast love and faithfulness."*

68. **1 John 4:9:** - *"In this the love of God was made manifest among us, that God sent his only Son into the world so that we might live through him."*

69. **Luke 6:27:** - *"But I say to you who hear, Love your enemies, do good to those who hate you."*

70. **Psalm 33:22:** - *"Let your steadfast love, O Lord, be upon us, even as we hope in you."*

71. **Psalm 145:9:** - *"The Lord is good to all, and his mercy is over all that he has made."*

72. **2 Thessalonians 3:3:** - *"But the Lord is faithful. He will establish you and guard you against the evil one."*

73. **Ephesians 5:2:** - *"And walk in love, as Christ loved us and gave himself up for us, a fragrant offering and sacrifice to God."*

74. **Psalm 100:5:** - *"For the Lord is good; his steadfast love endures forever, and his faithfulness to all generations."*

75. **1 John 4:8:** - *"Whoever does not love does not know God, because God is love."*

76. **Romans 12:9:** - *"Let love be genuine. Abhor what is evil; hold fast to what is good."*

77. **2 Thessalonians 3:5:** - *"May the Lord direct your hearts into the love of God and into the steadfastness of Christ."*

78. **1 John 3:16:** - *"By this we know love, that he laid down his life for us, and we ought to lay down our lives for the brothers."*

79. **1 John 4:7:** - *"Beloved, let us love one another, for love is from God, and whoever loves has been born of God and knows God."*

80. **1 John 4:21:** - *"And this commandment we have from him: whoever loves God must also love his brother."*

81. **Hebrews 6:10:** - *"For God is not unjust so as to overlook your work and the love that you have shown for his name in serving the saints, as you still do."*

82. **Romans 12:9:** - *"Let love be genuine. Abhor what is evil; hold fast to what is good."*

83. **Romans 8:38-39:** - *"For I am sure that neither death nor life, nor angels nor rulers, nor things present nor things to come, nor powers, nor height nor depth, nor anything else in all creation, will be able to separate us from the love of God in Christ Jesus our Lord."*

84. **Ephesians 2:4-5:** - *"But God, being rich in mercy, because*

of the great love with which he loved us, even when we were dead in our trespasses, made us alive together with Christ—by grace you have been saved."

85. **Romans 5:8:** - *"But God shows his love for us in that while we were still sinners, Christ died for us."*

86. **Psalm 86:15:** - *"For the Lord is good; his steadfast love endures forever, and his faithfulness to all generations."*

87. **Romans 5:5:** - *"And hope does not put us to shame, because God's love has been poured into our hearts through the Holy Spirit who has been given to us."*

88. **Romans 13:8:** - *"Owe no one anything, except to love each other, for the one who loves another has fulfilled the law."*

89. **1 Corinthians 16:14:** - *"Let all that you do be done in love."*

90. **Galatians 2:20:** - *"I have been crucified with Christ. It is no longer I who live, but Christ who lives in me. And the life I now live in the flesh I live by faith in the Son of God, who loved me and gave himself for me."*

91. **Zephaniah 3:17:** - *"The Lord your God is in your midst, a mighty one who will save; he will rejoice over you with gladness; he will quiet you by his love; he will exult over you with loud singing."*

92. **John 15:13:** - *"Greater love has no one than this, that someone lay down his life for his friends."*

93. **Psalm 143:8:** - *"Let the morning bring me word of your unfailing love, for I have put my trust in you. Show me the way I should go, for to you, I entrust my life."*

94. **Lamentations 3:22-23:** - *"The steadfast love of the Lord never ceases; his mercies never come to an end; they are new every morning; great is your faithfulness."*

95. **1 John 4:11:** - *"Beloved, if God so loved us, we also ought to love one another."*

96. **Ephesians 2:4-5 (NKJV):** - *"But God, who is rich in mercy, because of His great love with which He loved us, even when we were dead in trespasses, made us alive together with Christ (by grace you have been saved)."*

97. **Luke 6:27-28:** - *"But I say to you who hear, love your enemies, do good to those who hate you, bless those who curse you, pray for those who mistreat you."*

98. **John 13:34:** - *"A new commandment I give to you, that you love one another: just as I have loved you, you also are to love one another."*

99. **1 John 4:19:** - *"We love because he first loved us."*

100. **Colossians 3:14:** - *"And over all these virtues put on love, which binds them all together in perfect unity."*

3

BUSINESS AND FINANCE QUOTES

The chapter "Quotes Business and Finance" delves into timeless wisdom from scriptures relevant to business and finance. It explores principles such as stewardship, diligence, integrity, and the proper use of wealth, drawing upon biblical teachings. The quotes offer practical guidance and spiritual perspectives that can inspire and inform approaches to financial matters, catering to seasoned entrepreneurs, aspiring investors, and those seeking wisdom for resource management.

1. **Proverbs 16:3** - *"Commit to the Lord whatever you do, and he will establish your plans."*

2. **Proverbs 21:5** - *"The plans of the diligent lead to profit as surely as haste leads to poverty."*

3. **Luke 6:38** - *"Give, and it will be given to you. A good measure,*

pressed down, shaken together, and running over, will be poured into your lap. For with the measure you use, it will be measured to you."

4. **Proverbs 23:4** - *"Do not wear yourself out to get rich; do not trust your own cleverness.*"

5. **Proverbs 3:9** - *"Honor the Lord with your wealth, with the firstfruits of all your crops.*"

6. **Luke 16:10** - *"Whoever can be trusted with very little can also be trusted with much, and whoever is dishonest with very little will also be dishonest with much.*"

7. **Proverbs 10:22** - *"The blessing of the Lord brings wealth, without painful toil for it.*"

8. **Proverbs 13:11** - *"Dishonest money dwindles away, but whoever gathers money little by little makes it grow.*"

9. **Proverbs 11:25** - *"A generous person will prosper; whoever refreshes others will be refreshed.*"

10. **Psalm 49:16** - *"Do not be overawed when others grow rich, when the splendor of their houses increases.*"

11. **Proverbs 13:22** - *"A good person leaves an inheritance for their children's children, but a sinner's wealth is stored up for the righteous.*"

12. **Deuteronomy 28:12** - *"The Lord will open the heavens, the storehouse of his bounty, to send rain on your land in season and to bless all the work of your hands.*"

13. **Proverbs 20:13** - *"Do not love sleep or you will grow poor; stay awake and you will have food to spare."*

14. **Proverbs 21:5** - *"The plans of the diligent lead to profit as surely as haste leads to poverty."*

15. **Proverbs 28:20** - *"A faithful person will be richly blessed, but one eager to get rich will not go unpunished."*

16. **Proverbs 22:7** - *"The rich rule over the poor, and the borrower is slave to the lender."*

17. **Proverbs 27:23-24** - *"Be sure you know the condition of your flocks, give careful attention to your herds; for riches do not endure forever, and a crown is not secure for all generations."*

18. **Psalm 37:21** - *"The wicked borrow and do not repay, but the righteous give generously."*

19. **Proverbs 22:26-27** - *"Do not be one who shakes hands in pledge or puts up security for debts; if you lack the means to pay, your very bed will be snatched from under you."*

20. **Proverbs 10:4** - *"Lazy hands make for poverty, but diligent hands bring wealth."*

21. **Proverbs 13:8** - *"A person's riches may ransom their life, but the poor cannot respond to threatening rebukes."*

22. **Proverbs 11:4** - *"Wealth is worthless in the day of wrath, but righteousness delivers from death."*

23. **Proverbs 22:7** - *"The borrower is slave to the lender."*

24. **Proverbs 18:11** - *"The wealth of the rich is their fortified city; they imagine it a wall too high to scale."*

25. **Proverbs 11:25** - *"A generous person will prosper; whoever refreshes others will be refreshed."*

26. **Acts 20:35** - *"In everything I did, I showed you that by this kind of hard work we must help the weak, remembering the words the Lord Jesus himself said: 'It is more blessed to give than to receive.'"*

27. **Proverbs 22:22** - *"Do not exploit the poor because they are poor and do not crush the needy in court."*

28. **Proverbs 21:5** - *"The plans of the diligent lead to profit as surely as haste leads to poverty."*

29. **Proverbs 12:10** - *"The righteous care for the needs of their animals, but the kindest acts of the wicked are cruel."*

30. **Proverbs 11:1** - *"The Lord detests dishonest scales, but accurate weights find favor with him."*

31. **Proverbs 15:16** - *"Better a little with the fear of the Lord than great wealth with turmoil."*

32. **Proverbs 16:8** - *"Better a little with righteousness than much gain with injustice."*

33. **Proverbs 21:5** - *"The plans of the diligent lead to profit as surely as haste leads to poverty."*

34. **Proverbs 22:2** - *"The rich and the poor have this in common: The Lord is the Maker of them all."*

35. **Psalm 23:1** - *"The Lord is my shepherd, I lack nothing."*

36. **Proverbs 23:4** - *"Do not wear yourself out to get rich; do not trust your own cleverness."*

37. **Proverbs 30:8-9** - *"Keep falsehood and lies far from me; give me neither poverty nor riches, but give me only my daily bread."*

38. **Matthew 6:21** - *"For where your treasure is, there your heart will be also."*

39. **Proverbs 13:22** - *"A good person leaves an inheritance for their children's children, but a sinner's wealth is stored up for the righteous."*

40. **Proverbs 13:11** - *"Dishonest money dwindles away, but whoever gathers money little by little makes it grow."*

41. **Proverbs 15:16** - *"Better a little with the fear of the Lord than great wealth with turmoil."*

42. **Proverbs 21:5** - *"The plans of the diligent lead to profit as surely as haste leads to poverty."*

43. **Proverbs 3:9** - *"Honor the Lord with your wealth, with the firstfruits of all your crops."*

44. **Proverbs 28:20** - *"A faithful person will be richly blessed, but one eager to get rich will not go unpunished."*

45. **Proverbs 18:11** - *"The wealth of the rich is their fortified city; they imagine it a wall too high to scale."*

46. **Proverbs 22:22** - *"Do not exploit the poor because they are poor and do not crush the needy in court."*

47. **Proverbs 21:5** - *"The plans of the diligent lead to profit as surely as haste leads to poverty."*

48. **Hebrews 13:5** - *"Keep your lives free from the love of money and be content with what you have, because God has said, 'Never will I leave you; never will I forsake you.'"*

49. **Matthew 6:33** - *"But seek first his kingdom and his righteousness, and all these things will be given to you as well."*

50. **Proverbs 22:1** - *"A good name is more desirable than great riches; to be esteemed is better than silver or gold."*

51. **Philippians 4:6** - *"Do not be anxious about anything, but in every situation, by prayer and petition, with thanksgiving, present your requests to God."*

52. **1 Samuel 2:7** - *"The Lord makes poor and makes rich; he brings low, and he exalts."*

53. **Psalm 37:21** - *"The wicked borrows but does not pay back, but the righteous is generous and gives."*

54. **1 Timothy 6:9** - *"But those who want to get rich fall into temptation and a snare and many foolish and harmful desires which plunge men into ruin and destruction."*

55. **Proverbs 28:22** - *"A stingy man hastens after wealth and does not know that poverty will come upon him."*

56. **Proverbs 16:1** - *"The plans of the heart belong to man, but the answer of the tongue is from the Lord."*

57. **Proverbs 16:8** - *"Better is a little with righteousness than great revenues with injustice."*

58. **Proverbs 22:16** - *"Whoever oppresses the poor to increase his own wealth, or gives to the rich, will only come to poverty."*

59. **Deuteronomy 28:12** - *"The Lord will open to you his good treasury, the heavens, to give the rain to your land in its season and to bless all the work of your hands."*

60. **Proverbs 10:4** - *"A slack hand causes poverty, but the hand of the diligent makes rich."*

61. **Proverbs 3:27** - *"Do not withhold good from those to whom it is due, when it is in your power to act."*

62. **Proverbs 21:5** - *"The plans of the diligent lead surely to abundance, but everyone who is hasty comes only to poverty."*

63. **Romans 14:23** - *"But whoever has doubts is condemned if they eat, because their eating is not from faith; and everything that does not come from faith is sin."*

64. **Matthew 6:24** - *"No one can serve two masters. Either you will hate the one and love the other, or you will be devoted to the one and despise the other. You cannot serve both God and money."*

65. **Proverbs 14:23** - *"In all toil there is profit, but mere talk tends only to poverty."*

66. **Psalm 23:1** - *"The Lord is my shepherd; I shall not want."*

67. **Mark 8:36** - *"For what does it profit a man to gain the whole world and forfeit his soul?"*

68. **Matthew 6:21** - *"For where your treasure is, there your heart will be also."*

69. **Proverbs 22:7** - *"The rich rules over the poor, and the borrower is the slave of the lender."*

70. **Proverbs 6:10-11** - *"A little sleep, a little slumber, a little folding of the hands to rest, and poverty will come upon you like a robber, and want like an armed man."*

71. **Deuteronomy 8:18** - *"But you shall remember the Lord your God, for it is he who gives you power to get wealth."*

72. **Proverbs 15:16** - *"Better is a little with the fear of the Lord than great treasure and trouble with it."*

73. **Proverbs 10:22** - *"The blessing of the Lord makes rich, and he adds no sorrow with it."*

74. **Ephesians 4:28** - *"Let the thief no longer steal, but rather let him labor, doing honest work with his own hands, so that he may have something to share with anyone in need."*

4

QUOTES FOR POLITICS

"Quotes for Politics" guides readers through a journey of timeless wisdom, exploring the relationship between faith and governance. Drawing from biblical scriptures, the chapter sheds light on how divine guidance applies to navigating political complexities. Each quote emphasizes principles like justice, mercy, leadership, and governance, offering clarity and inspiration to those striving to improve societies. Through these passages, readers uncover insights into effective governance and timeless truths that transcend cultural and temporal boundaries. Ultimately, "Quotes for Politics" underscores the enduring relevance of biblical wisdom in fostering a more just, compassionate, and equitable world.

1. **Isaiah 33:22** - *"For the Lord is our judge, the Lord is our lawgiver, the Lord is our king; he will save us."*

2. **Psalm 33:12** - *"Blessed is the nation whose God is the Lord, the people he chose for his inheritance."*

3. **Exodus 18:21** - *"But select capable men from all the people—men who fear God, trustworthy men who hate dishonest gain—and appoint them as officials over thousands, hundreds, fifties and tens."*

4. **Proverbs 14:34** - *"Righteousness exalts a nation, but sin condemns any people."*

5. **2 Chronicles 7:14** - *"If my people, who are called by my name, will humble themselves and pray and seek my face and turn from their wicked ways, then I will hear from heaven, and I will forgive their sin and will heal their land."*

6. **Romans 13:1** - *"Let everyone be subject to the governing authorities, for there is no authority except that which God has established."*

7. **Proverbs 21:1** - *"The king's heart is a stream of water in the hand of the Lord; he turns it wherever he will."*

8. **Proverbs 31:8** - *"Speak up for those who cannot speak for themselves, for the rights of all who are destitute."*

9. **Isaiah 10:1** - *"Woe to those who make unjust laws, to those who issue oppressive decrees."*

10. **Matthew 22:21** - *"Give to Caesar what is Caesar's, and to God what is God's."*

11. **Romans 13:1** - *"Let every person be subject to the governing authorities. For there is no authority except from God, and those that exist have been instituted by God."*

12. **Proverbs 29:2** - *"When the righteous thrive, the people rejoice; when the wicked rule, the people groan."*

13. **Jeremiah 29:7** - *"But seek the welfare of the city where I have sent you into exile, and pray to the Lord on its behalf, for in its welfare you will find your welfare."*

14. **Proverbs 31:8** - *"Open your mouth for the mute, for the rights of all who are destitute."*

15. **Proverbs 11:3** - *"The integrity of the upright guides them, but the unfaithful are destroyed by their duplicity."*

16. **Romans 12:21** - *"Do not be overcome by evil, but overcome evil with good."*

17. **Proverbs 29:4** - *"By justice a king gives a country stability, but those who are greedy for bribes tear it down."*

18. **Proverbs 20:26** - *"A wise king winnows out the wicked; he drives the threshing wheel over them."*

19. **Proverbs 28:2** - *"When a land transgresses, it has many rulers, but with a man of understanding and knowledge, its stability will long continue."*

20. **Deuteronomy 16:19** - *"Do not pervert justice or show partiality. Do not accept a bribe, for a bribe blinds the eyes of the wise and twists the words of the innocent."*

21. **Proverbs 16:12** - *"It is an abomination for kings to do evil, for the throne is established by righteousness."*

22. **Proverbs 11:1** - *"The Lord detests dishonest scales, but accurate weights find favor with him."*

23. **Proverbs 17:23** - *"The wicked accept bribes in secret to pervert the course of justice."*

24. **Proverbs 22:22** - *"Do not rob the poor because he is poor, or crush the afflicted at the gate."*

25. **Psalm 72:2** - *"May he judge your people in righteousness, your afflicted ones with justice."*

26. **Proverbs 29:13** - *"The poor and the oppressor have this in common: The Lord gives sight to the eyes of both."*

27. **Isaiah 1:17** - *"Learn to do right; seek justice. Defend the oppressed. Take up the cause of the fatherless; plead the case of the widow."*

28. **Proverbs 29:2** - *"When the righteous increase, the people rejoice, but when the wicked rule, the people groan."*

29. **Proverbs 10:11** - *"The mouth of the righteous is a fountain of life, but the mouth of the wicked conceals violence."*

30. **Proverbs 29:4** - *"The king gives stability to the land by justice, but a man who takes bribes overthrows it."*

31. **Micah 6:8** - *"He has told you, O man, what is good; and what does the Lord require of you but to do justice, and to love kindness, and to walk humbly with your God?"*

32. **Isaiah 10:1** - *"Woe to those who decree iniquitous decrees, and the writers who keep writing oppression."*

33. **Proverbs 29:4** - *"By justice a king builds up the land, but he who exacts gifts tears it down."*

34. **Proverbs 3:27** - *"Do not withhold good from those to whom it is due, when it is in your power to act."*

35. **Proverbs 19:17** - *"Whoever is generous to the poor lends to the Lord, and he will repay him for his deed."*

36. **Proverbs 11:1** - *"A false balance is an abomination to the Lord, but a just weight is his delight."*

37. **Proverbs 21:13** - *"Whoever closes his ear to the cry of the poor will himself call out and not be answered."*

38. **Proverbs 29:12** - *"If a ruler listens to falsehood, all his officials will be wicked."*

39. **Romans 13:1** - *"Let every person be subject to the governing authorities. For there is no authority except from God, and those that exist have been instituted by God."*

40. **Deuteronomy 24:17** - *"You shall not pervert the justice due to the sojourner or to the fatherless, or take a widow's garment in pledge."*

41. **Proverbs 21:3** - *"To do righteousness and justice is more acceptable to the Lord than sacrifice."*

42. **Proverbs 12:15** - *"The way of a fool is right in his own eyes, but a wise man listens to advice."*

43. **Proverbs 14:31** - *"Whoever oppresses the poor shows contempt for their Maker, but whoever is kind to the needy honors God."*

44. **Proverbs 28:16** - *"A ruler who lacks understanding is a cruel oppressor, but he who hates unjust gain will prolong his days."*

45. **Proverbs 21:15** - *"When justice is done, it brings joy to the righteous but terror to evildoers."*

46. **Proverbs 14:35** - *"The king's favor is toward a wise servant, but his wrath is against him who causes shame."*

47. **Proverbs 28:16** - *"The prince who lacks understanding is also a great oppressor, but he who hates unjust gain will prolong his days."*

48. **Psalm 9:9** - *"The Lord is a refuge for the oppressed, a stronghold in times of trouble."*

49. **Amos 5:24** - *"Let justice roll down like waters, and righteousness like an ever-flowing stream."*

50. **Proverbs 21:21** - *"Whoever pursues righteousness and kindness will find life, righteousness, and honor."*

51. **Proverbs 28:1** - *"The wicked flee when no one pursues, but the righteous are bold as a lion."*

52. **Proverbs 16:12** - *"It is an abomination to kings to do evil, for the throne is established by righteousness."*

53. **Proverbs 29:7** - *"The righteous care about justice for the poor, but the wicked have no such concern."*

54. **Amos 5:24** - *"But let justice roll down like waters, and righteousness like an ever-flowing stream."*

55. **Proverbs 22:8** - *"Whoever sows injustice will reap calamity, and the rod of his fury will fail."*

56. **Proverbs 16:8** - *"Better is a little with righteousness than great revenues with injustice."*

57. **Proverbs 28:21** - *"To show partiality is not good, but for a piece of bread a man will do wrong."*

58. **Proverbs 14:20** - *"The poor is disliked even by his neighbor, but the rich has many friends."*

59. **Proverbs 28:5** - *"Evil men do not understand justice, but those who seek the Lord understand it completely."*

60. **Proverbs 29:12** - *"A ruler who listens to lies will have all his officials wicked."*

61. **John 7:24** - *"Do not judge by appearances, but judge with right judgment."*

62. **Proverbs 29:7** - *"A righteous man knows the rights of the poor; a wicked man does not understand such knowledge."*

63. **Proverbs 22:16** - *"He who oppresses the poor to increase his wealth and he who gives gifts to the rich—both come to poverty."*

5

QUOTES FOR MARRIAGE

This chapter celebrates the sacred institution of marriage, which has endured across cultures and faiths throughout history. It explores timeless wisdom from the Bible, offering guidance, inspiration, and comfort for those entering into marriage or seeking to strengthen their existing union. Through verses, the chapter delves into fundamental principles, virtues, and practices essential for a fulfilling and lasting marriage, drawing upon the wisdom of scripture. Whether preparing for marriage, navigating its challenges, or deepening one's understanding of this divine covenant, "Quotes for Marriage" provides valuable insights and encouragement rooted in the eternal truths of the Bible.

1. **Mark 10:9** - *"Therefore what God has joined together, let no one separate."*

2. **1 Corinthians 13:4** - *"Love is patient, love is kind. It does not envy, it does not boast, it is not proud."*

3. **Proverbs 12:4** - *"A wife of noble character is her husband's crown, but a disgraceful wife is like decay in his bones."*

4. **Ecclesiastes 4:9** - *"Two are better than one, because they have a good return for their labor."*

5. **Ephesians 5:25** - *"Husbands, love your wives, just as Christ loved the church and gave himself up for her."*

6. **Ecclesiastes 9:9** - *"Enjoy life with your wife, whom you love, all the days of this meaningless life that God has given you under the sun—all your meaningless days. For this is your lot in life and in your toilsome labor under the sun."*

7. **1 Peter 4:8** - *"Above all, love each other deeply, because love covers over a multitude of sins."*

8. **1 Corinthians 7:3** - *"Let the husband render to his wife the affection due her, and likewise also the wife to her husband."*

9. **Ecclesiastes 4:12** - *"A cord of three strands is not quickly broken."*

10. **Ephesians 5:22** - *"Wives, submit yourselves to your own husbands as you do to the Lord."*

11. **Ephesians 5:31** - *"For this reason, a man will leave his father and mother and be united to his wife, and the two will become one flesh."*

12. **Mark 10:6-7** - *"But from the beginning of creation, 'God made them male and female.' Therefore a man shall leave his father and mother and hold fast to his wife.'"*

13. **Ephesians 4:2** - *"Be completely humble and gentle; be patient, bearing with one another in love."*

14. **Colossians 3:19** - *"Husbands, love your wives and do not be harsh with them."*

15. **Proverbs 5:18** - *"May your fountain be blessed, and may you rejoice in the wife of your youth."*

16. **Ephesians 5:28** - *"In the same way, husbands ought to love their wives as their own bodies. He who loves his wife loves himself."*

17. **Proverbs 20:24** - *"A man's steps are directed by the Lord. How then can anyone understand their own way?"*

18. **John 15:12** - *"Love one another as I have loved you."*

19. **Hebrews 13:4** - *"Let marriage be held in honor among all, and let the marriage bed be undefiled, for God will judge the sexually immoral and adulterous."*

20. **Proverbs 17:17** - *"A friend loves at all times, and a brother is born for a time of adversity."*

21. **Colossians 3:14** - *"And over all these virtues put on love, which binds them all together in perfect unity."*

22. **Proverbs 10:12** - *"Hatred stirs up conflict, but love covers over all wrongs."*

23. **Philippians 4:6** - *"Do not be anxious about anything, but in every situation, by prayer and petition, with thanksgiving, present your requests to God."*

24. **Galatians 5:22-23** - *"But the fruit of the Spirit is love, joy, peace, forbearance, kindness, goodness, faithfulness, gentleness, and self-control. Against such things, there is no law."*

25. **Ephesians 5:25 (NLT)** - *"A husband's love should be like the love of the Lord, pure and eternal."*

26. **1 Peter 3:1** - *"Wives, in the same way, submit yourselves to your own husbands so that, if any of them do not believe the word, they may be won over without words by the behavior of their wives."*

27. **Ruth 1:16** - *"For where you go, I will go, and where you lodge, I will lodge. Your people shall be my people, and your God my God."*

28. **Proverbs 31:30** - *"Charm is deceptive, and beauty is fleeting; but a woman who fears the Lord is to be praised."*

29. **2 Thessalonians 3:3** - *"But the Lord is faithful, and he will strengthen you and protect you from the evil one."*

30. **John 13:34** - *"A new command I give you: Love one another. As I have loved you, so you must love one another."*

31. **Proverbs 18:22** - *"A man who finds a wife finds a good thing and obtains favor from the Lord."*

32. **Ephesians 4:29** - *"Do not let any unwholesome talk come*

out of your mouths, but only what is helpful for building others up according to their needs, that it may benefit those who listen."

33. **Matthew 19:6** - *"Therefore, what God has joined together, let no one separate."*

34. **Proverbs 18:22** - *"He who finds a wife finds what is good and receives favor from the Lord."*

35. **Matthew 5:32** - *"But I say to you that everyone who divorces his wife, except on the ground of sexual immorality, makes her commit adultery, and whoever marries a divorced woman commits adultery."*

36. **Ephesians 5:33** - *"However, let each one of you love his wife as himself, and let the wife see that she respects her husband."*

37. **1 Timothy 5:8** - *"But if anyone does not provide for his relatives, and especially for members of his household, he has denied the faith and is worse than an unbeliever."*

38. **Colossians 3:12** - *"Therefore, as God's chosen people, holy and dearly loved, clothe yourselves with compassion, kindness, humility, gentleness, and patience."*

39. **1 Corinthians 15:33** - *"Do not be deceived: 'Bad company ruins good morals.'"*

40. **Ephesians 5:25** - *"Husbands, love your wives, as Christ loved the church and gave himself up for her."*

41. **James 3:17** - *"But the wisdom that comes from heaven is first of all pure; then peace-loving, considerate, submissive, full of mercy and good fruit, impartial, and sincere."*

41

42. **Proverbs 12:4** - *"An excellent wife is the crown of her husband, but she who brings shame is like rottenness in his bones."*

43. **2 Corinthians 6:14** - *"Do not be unequally yoked with unbelievers. For what partnership has righteousness with lawlessness? Or what fellowship has light with darkness?"*

44. **1 Corinthians 13:6** - *"Love does not delight in evil but rejoices with the truth."*

45. **Proverbs 15:1** - *"A soft answer turns away wrath, but a harsh word stirs up anger."*

46. **1 Peter 4:8** - *"Above all, keep loving one another earnestly, since love covers a multitude of sins."*

47. **1 Corinthians 6:18** - *"Flee from sexual immorality. Every other sin a person commits is outside the body, but the sexually immoral person sins against his own body."*

48. **Colossians 3:16** - *"Let the word of Christ dwell in you richly, teaching and admonishing one another in all wisdom, singing psalms and hymns and spiritual songs, with thankfulness in your hearts to God."*

49. **Ephesians 5:25 (NLT)** - *"For husbands, this means love your wives, just as Christ loved the church. He gave up his life for her."*

50. **2 Thessalonians 3:3** - *"But the Lord is faithful. He will establish you and guard you against the evil one."*

51. **Proverbs 16:9** - *"A man's heart plans his way, but the Lord directs his steps."*

52. **1 John 4:7** - *"Beloved, let us love one another, for love is from God, and whoever loves has been born of God and knows God."*

53. **Proverbs 3:3** - *"Let not steadfast love and faithfulness forsake you; bind them around your neck; write them on the tablet of your heart."*

54. **Colossians 3:12** - *"Put on then, as God's chosen ones, holy and beloved, compassionate hearts, kindness, humility, meekness, and patience."*

55. **Proverbs 13:20** - *"He who walks with the wise grows wise, but a companion of fools suffers harm."*

56. **Proverbs 3:27** - *"Do not withhold good from those to whom it is due, when it is in your power to act."*

57. **Proverbs 15:18** - *"A hot-tempered person stirs up conflict, but the one who is patient calms a quarrel."*

58. **Proverbs 29:11** - *"A fool gives full vent to his spirit, but a wise man quietly holds it back."*

59. **Colossians 3:14** - *"And above all these put on love, which binds everything together in perfect harmony."*

60. **Ephesians 4:32** - *"Be kind to one another, tenderhearted, forgiving one another, as God in Christ forgave you."*

61. **Proverbs 17:22** - *"A joyful heart is good medicine, but a crushed spirit dries up the bones."*

62. **Galatians 5:22-23** - *"But the fruit of the Spirit is love, joy, peace, patience, kindness, goodness, faithfulness, gentleness, self-control; against such things, there is no law."*

63. **Proverbs 17:17** - *"A friend loves at all times, and a brother is born for adversity."*

64. **Proverbs 16:9** - *"The heart of man plans his way, but the Lord establishes his steps."*

65. **1 John 4:18** - *"There is no fear in love, but perfect love casts out fear. For fear has to do with punishment, and whoever fears has not been perfected in love."*

66. **Psalm 23:1** - *"The Lord is my shepherd; I shall not want."*

67. **1 Corinthians 13:13** - *"So now faith, hope, and love abide, these three; but the greatest of these is love."*

68. **Proverbs 25:11** - *"A word fitly spoken is like apples of gold in a setting of silver."*

69. **Romans 8:28** - *"And we know that in all things God works for the good of those who love him, who have been called according to his purpose."*

70. **Proverbs 25:28** - *"A man who does not control his temper is like a city whose wall is broken down."*

71. **Numbers 6:24-25** - *"The Lord bless you and keep you; the Lord make his face shine on you and be gracious to you."*

72. **Proverbs 18:22** - *"He who finds a wife finds what is good and receives favor from the Lord."*

73. **Jeremiah 29:11** - *"For I know the plans I have for you, declares the Lord, plans for welfare and not for evil, to give you a future and a hope."*

74. **Proverbs 16:24** - *"Pleasant words are a honeycomb, sweet to the soul and healing to the bones."*

75. **Proverbs 31:10** - *"An excellent wife who can find? She is far more precious than jewels."*

76. **1 Samuel 16:7** - *"But the Lord said to Samuel, 'Do not look on his appearance or on the height of his stature, because I have rejected him. For the Lord sees not as man sees: man looks on the outward appearance, but the Lord looks on the heart.'"*

77. **Proverbs 20:7** - *"The righteous who walks in his integrity— blessed are his children after him!"*

78. **Proverbs 16:3** - *"Commit your work to the Lord, and your plans will be established."*

79. **James 1:25** - *"But the one who looks into the perfect law, the law of liberty, and perseveres, being no hearer who forgets but a doer who acts, he will be blessed in his doing."*

80. **Proverbs 15:4** - *"A gentle tongue is a tree of life, but perverseness in it breaks the spirit."*

81. **Galatians 6:9** - *"And let us not grow weary of doing good, for in due season we will reap, if we do not give up."*

82. **Proverbs 18:24** - *"A man of many companions may come to ruin, but there is a friend who sticks closer than a brother."*

83. **Romans 12:2** - *"Do not be conformed to this world, but be transformed by the renewal of your mind, that by testing you may discern what is the will of God, what is good and acceptable and perfect."*

84. **Proverbs 15:1** - *"A soft answer turns away wrath, but a harsh word stirs up anger."*

85. **1 Samuel 16:7** - *"But the Lord said to Samuel, 'Do not look on his appearance or on the height of his stature, because I have rejected him. For the Lord sees not as man sees: man looks on the outward appearance, but the Lord looks on the heart.'"*

86. **Proverbs 29:11** - *"A fool gives full vent to his spirit, but a wise man quietly holds it back."*

87. **Ephesians 4:32** - *"Be kind to one another, tenderhearted, forgiving one another, as God in Christ forgave you."*

88. **Proverbs 16:9** - *"A man's heart plans his way, but the Lord directs his steps."*

89. **Proverbs 3:3** - *"Let love and faithfulness never leave you; bind them around your neck, write them on the tablet of your heart."*

90. **Psalm 23:1** - *"The Lord is my shepherd; I shall not want."*

91. **Proverbs 12:15** - *"A wise man listens to advice."*

92. **Romans 12:10** - *"Love one another with brotherly affection. Outdo one another in showing honor."*

93. **Psalm 145:18** - *"The Lord is near to all who call on him, to all who call on him in truth."*

94. **Philippians 4:6** - *"Do not be anxious about anything, but in everything by prayer and supplication with thanksgiving let your requests be made known to God."*

95. **Proverbs 31:10** - *"A wife of noble character who can find? She is worth far more than rubies."*

96. **1 Thessalonians 5:11** - *"Therefore encourage one another and build one another up, just as you are doing."*

97. **Romans 15:13** - *"May the God of hope fill you with all joy and peace in believing, so that by the power of the Holy Spirit you may abound in hope."*

98. **1 Corinthians 16:14** - *"Let everything you do be done in love."*

6

QUOTES FOR CHILDREN

"Quotes for Children" is a captivating section within the compilation, designed to offer timeless wisdom and moral guidance for young minds. Through carefully chosen quotes from the Bible, children are encouraged to explore foundational principles that shape character and inspire growth. Each quote is crafted to resonate with the innocence and curiosity of childhood, fostering understanding of values like love, compassion, and integrity. This section serves as a beacon of light, guiding children towards a purposeful life rooted in faith and virtue.

1. **Proverbs 22:6** - *"Train up a child in the way he should go; even when he is old he will not depart from it."*

2. **Colossians 3:20** - *"Children, obey your parents in everything, for this pleases the Lord."*

3. **Philippians 4:13** - *"I can do all things through him who strengthens me."*

4. **Psalm 23:1** - *"The Lord is my shepherd; I shall not want."*

5. **Matthew 19:14** - *"Let the little children come to me and do not hinder them, for to such belongs the kingdom of heaven."*

6. **Jeremiah 29:11** - *"For I know the plans I have for you, declares the Lord, plans for welfare and not for evil, to give you a future and a hope."*

7. **Philippians 4:6** - *"Do not be anxious about anything, but in everything by prayer and supplication with thanksgiving let your requests be made known to God."*

8. **Matthew 19:14** - *"But Jesus said, 'Let the little children come to me and do not hinder them, for to such belongs the kingdom of heaven.'"*

9. **Genesis 1:1** - *"In the beginning, God created the heavens and the earth."*

10. **Proverbs 1:7** - *"The fear of the Lord is the beginning of knowledge; fools despise wisdom and instruction."*

11. **Psalm 139:14** - *"I praise you, for I am fearfully and wonderfully made. Wonderful are your works; my soul knows it very well."*

12. **John 14:6** - *"Jesus said to him, 'I am the way, and the truth, and the life. No one comes to the Father except through me.'"*

13. **Romans 12:2** - *"Do not be conformed to this world, but be*

transformed by the renewal of your mind, that by testing you may discern what is the will of God, what is good and acceptable and perfect."

14. **Numbers 6:24-25** - *"The Lord bless you and keep you; the Lord make his face to shine upon you and be gracious to you."*

15. **2 Timothy 1:7** - *"For God gave us a spirit not of fear but of power and love and self-control."*

16. **Galatians 5:22** - *"But the fruit of the Spirit is love, joy, peace, patience, kindness, goodness, faithfulness."*

17. **Proverbs 3:5** - *"Trust in the Lord with all your heart, and do not lean on your own understanding."*

18. **John 15:5** - *"I am the vine; you are the branches. Whoever abides in me and I in him, he it is that bears much fruit, for apart from me you can do nothing."*

19. **Romans 8:28** - *"And we know that in all things God works for the good of those who love him, who have been called according to his purpose."*

20. **Romans 8:38-39** - *"For I am sure that neither death nor life, nor angels nor rulers, nor things present nor things to come, nor powers, nor height nor depth, nor anything else in all creation, will be able to separate us from the love of God in Christ Jesus our Lord."*

21. **Psalm 119:15** - *"I will meditate on your precepts and fix my eyes on your ways."*

22. **Psalm 145:9 -** *"The Lord is good to all, and his mercy is over all that he has made."*

23. **1 Timothy 4:12 -** *"Let no one despise you for your youth, but set the believers an example in speech, in conduct, in love, in faith, in purity."*

24. **1 John 5:14 -** *"And we are confident that he hears us whenever we ask for anything that pleases him."*

25. **Ephesians 2:8 -** *"For by grace you have been saved through faith. And this is not your own doing; it is the gift of God."*

26. **Isaiah 40:11 -** *"He tends his flock like a shepherd: He gathers the lambs in his arms and carries them close to his heart; he gently leads those that have young."*

27. **Deuteronomy 31:6 -** *"Be strong and courageous. Do not fear or be in dread of them, for it is the Lord your God who goes with you. He will not leave you or forsake you."*

28. **Isaiah 41:10 -** *"So do not fear, for I am with you; do not be dismayed, for I am your God. I will strengthen you and help you; I will uphold you with my righteous right hand."*

29. **Zephaniah 3:17 -** *"The Lord your God is with you, the Mighty Warrior who saves. He will take great delight in you; in his love, he will no longer rebuke you, but will rejoice over you with singing."*

30. **2 Corinthians 9:8 -** *"And God is able to bless you abundantly, so that in all things at all times, having all that you need, you will abound in every good work."*

31. **Isaiah 40:29 -** *"He gives strength to the weary and increases the power of the weak."*

32. **Psalm 18:2 -** *"The Lord is my rock, my fortress and my deliverer; my God is my rock, in whom I take refuge, my shield and the horn of my salvation, my stronghold."*

33. **Psalm 86:15 -** *"But you, Lord, are a compassionate and gracious God, slow to anger, abounding in love and faithfulness."*

34. **Psalm 143:8 -** *"Let the morning bring me word of your unfailing love, for I have put my trust in you. Show me the way I should go, for to you I entrust my life."*

35. **Philippians 4:7 -** *"And the peace of God, which transcends all understanding, will guard your hearts and your minds in Christ Jesus."*

36. **Exodus 15:2 -** *"The Lord is my strength and my song; he has become my salvation."*

37. **Isaiah 41:13 -** *"For I am the Lord your God who takes hold of your right hand and says to you, 'Do not fear; I will help you.'"*

38. **Psalm 9:1** - *"I will praise you, Lord, with all my heart; I will tell of all the marvelous things you have done."*

39. **Psalm 119:105 -** *"Your word is a lamp for my feet, a light on my path."*

40. **Psalm 150:6 -** *"Let everything that has breath praise the Lord. Praise the Lord."*

41. **Matthew 6:33** - *"But seek first his kingdom and his righteousness, and all these things will be given to you as well."*

42. **John 14:18** - *"I will not leave you as orphans; I will come to you."*

43. **Zephaniah 3:17** - *"For the Lord your God is living among you. He is a mighty savior. He will take delight in you with gladness. With his love, he will calm all your fears. He will rejoice over you with joyful songs."*

44. **Matthew 28:20** - *"I am with you always, to the end of the age."*

7

QUOTES FOR SIN

In this chapter, readers explore sin's complexities through selected biblical verses. It delves into sin's nature, consequences, and paths to redemption across the Old and New Testaments. The included quotes offer insights into humanity's struggle with sin and the guidance towards repentance and spiritual growth. The chapter serves as a poignant reminder of the universal human condition and the enduring hope found in faith, making it valuable for personal reflection and understanding of biblical principles.

1. **1 John 1:9 -** *"If we confess our sins, he is faithful and just to forgive us our sins and to cleanse us from all unrighteousness."*

2. **Matthew 6:15 -** *"But if you do not forgive others their sins, your Father will not forgive your sins."*

3. **2 Corinthians 5:17 -** *"Therefore, if anyone is in Christ, the new creation has come: The old has gone, the new is here!"*

4. **1 Corinthians 6:18** - *"Flee from sexual immorality. All other sins a person commits are outside the body, but whoever sins sexually, sins against their own body."*

5. **Romans 6:23** - *"For the wages of sin is death, but the gift of God is eternal life in Christ Jesus our Lord."*

6. **Galatians 6:7** - *"Do not be deceived: God cannot be mocked. A man reaps what he sows."*

7. **James 4:7** - *"Submit yourselves therefore to God. Resist the devil, and he will flee from you."*

8. **Galatians 5:16** - *"But I say, walk by the Spirit, and you will not gratify the desires of the flesh."*

9. **2 Peter 3:9** - *"The Lord is not slow to fulfill his promise as some count slowness, but is patient toward you, not wishing that any should perish, but that all should reach repentance."*

10. **Acts 3:19** - *"Repent, then, and turn to God, so that your sins may be wiped out, that times of refreshing may come from the Lord."*

11. **Romans 3:23** - *"For all have sinned and fall short of the glory of God."*

12. **1 John 1:10** - *"If we say we have not sinned, we make him a liar, and his word is not in us."*

13. **Galatians 6:8** - *"For the one who sows to his own flesh will from the flesh reap corruption, but the one who sows to the Spirit will from the Spirit reap eternal life."*

14. **Jeremiah 17:9** - *"The heart is deceitful above all things, and desperately sick; who can understand it?"*

15. **Ephesians 4:32** - *"Be kind to one another, tenderhearted, forgiving one another, as God in Christ forgave you."*

16. **Romans 13:14** - *"But put on the Lord Jesus Christ, and make no provision for the flesh, to gratify its desires."*

17. **Romans 8:7** - *"For the mind that is set on the flesh is hostile to God, for it does not submit to God's law; indeed, it cannot."*

18. **Proverbs 28:13** - *"Whoever conceals their sins does not prosper, but the one who confesses and renounces them finds mercy."*

19. **Galatians 6:1** - *"Brothers, if anyone is caught in any transgression, you who are spiritual should restore him in a spirit of gentleness. Keep watch on yourself, lest you too be tempted."*

20. **Acts 3:19** - *"Repent therefore, and turn back, that your sins may be blotted out."*

21. **Romans 6:12** - *"Let not sin therefore reign in your mortal body, to make you obey its passions."*

22. **1 Corinthians 9:27** - *"But I discipline my body and keep it under control, lest after preaching to others I myself should be disqualified."*

23. **Psalm 51:2** - *"Wash me thoroughly from my iniquity, and cleanse me from my sin!"*

24. **1 Corinthians 10:13** - *"No temptation has overtaken you*

that is not common to man. God is faithful, and he will not let you be tempted beyond your ability, but with the temptation, he will also provide the way of escape, that you may be able to endure it."

25. **2 Corinthians 10:4** - *"For the weapons of our warfare are not of the flesh but have divine power to destroy strongholds."*

26. **Matthew 6:14** - *"For if you forgive others their trespasses, your heavenly Father will also forgive you."*

27. **Ephesians 5:3** - *"But among you, there must not be even a hint of sexual immorality, or of any kind of impurity, or of greed, because these are improper for God's holy people."*

28. **Psalm 32:1** - *"Blessed is the one whose transgression is forgiven, whose sin is covered."*

29. **Psalm 51:10** - *"Create in me a clean heart, O God, and renew a right spirit within me."*

30. **Galatians 6:7** - *"Do not be deceived: God is not mocked, for whatever one sows, that will he also reap."*

31. **John 3:36** - *"Whoever believes in the Son has eternal life; whoever does not obey the Son shall not see life, but the wrath of God remains on him."*

32. **Proverbs 28:13** - *"Whoever conceals his transgressions will not prosper, but he who confesses and forsakes them will obtain mercy."*

33. **Matthew 15:19** - *"For out of the heart come evil thoughts, murder, adultery, sexual immorality, theft, false witness, slander."*

34. **Matthew 5:28** - *"But I say to you that everyone who looks at a woman with lustful intent has already committed adultery with her in his heart."*

35. **Proverbs 4:19** - *"The way of the wicked is like deep darkness; they do not know over what they stumble."*

36. **Ephesians 4:30** - *"And do not grieve the Holy Spirit of God, by whom you were sealed for the day of redemption."*

37. **1 John 1:6** - *"If we say we have fellowship with him while we walk in darkness, we lie and do not practice the truth."*

38. **1 Peter 5:8** - *"Be sober-minded; be watchful. Your adversary, the devil, prowls around like a roaring lion, seeking someone to devour."*

39. **Galatians 5:16** - *"But I say, walk by the Spirit, and you will not gratify the desires of the flesh."*

40. **1 Thessalonians 4:7** - *"For God has not called us for impurity, but in holiness."*

41. **Romans 6:12** - *"Let not sin therefore reign in your mortal body, to make you obey its passions."*

42. **Matthew 5:29** - *"If your right eye causes you to sin, tear it out and throw it away. For it is better that you lose one of your members than that your whole body be thrown into hell."*

43. **Matthew 5:44** - *"But I say to you, Love your enemies and pray for those who persecute you."*

44. **1 John 3:8** - *"Whoever makes a practice of sinning is of the*

devil, for the devil has been sinning from the beginning. The reason the Son of God appeared was to destroy the works of the devil."

45. **Isaiah 55:7** - *"Let the wicked forsake his way, and the unrighteous man his thoughts; let him return to the Lord, that he may have compassion on him, and to our God, for he will abundantly pardon."*

46. **2 Peter 3:9** - *"The Lord is not slow to fulfill his promise as some count slowness, but is patient toward you, not wishing that any should perish, but that all should reach repentance."*

47. **James 5:16** - *"Therefore, confess your sins to one another and pray for one another, that you may be healed. The prayer of a righteous person has great power as it is working."*

48. **Romans 8:7** - *"For the mind that is set on the flesh is hostile to God, for it does not submit to God's law; indeed, it cannot."*

49. **Romans 12:21** - *"Do not be overcome by evil, but overcome evil with good."*

50. **Romans 6:22** - *"But now that you have been set free from sin and have become slaves of God, the fruit you get leads to sanctification and its end, eternal life."*

51. **Proverbs 10:9** - *"Whoever walks in integrity walks securely, but whoever takes crooked paths will be found out."*

52. **Mark 7:20-23** - *"And he said, What comes out of a person is what defiles him. For from within, out of the heart of man, come evil thoughts, sexual immorality, theft, murder, adultery, coveting, wickedness, deceit, sensuality, envy, slander, pride, foolishness. All these evil things come from within, and they defile a person."'*

8

QUOTES FOR REPENTANCE

"Quotes for Repentance" is a pivotal chapter that guides readers through a profound exploration of repentance in Christianity. Drawing from biblical wisdom, it illuminates the transformative power of acknowledging wrongdoing, seeking forgiveness, and embracing spiritual renewal. Carefully selected quotes encourage introspection, humility, and a deeper connection with the divine, fostering reconciliation with oneself and with God. This chapter offers timeless wisdom to navigate personal reflection and spiritual reckoning, nurturing a profound sense of reconciliation amidst life's complexities.

1. **Acts 2:38** - *"And Peter said to them, 'Repent and be baptized every one of you in the name of Jesus Christ for the forgiveness of your sins, and you will receive the gift of the Holy Spirit.'"*

2. **Acts 3:19** - *"Repent, then, and turn to God, so that your sins may be wiped out, that times of refreshing may come from the Lord."*

3. **Acts 8:22** - *"Repent of this wickedness and pray to the Lord in the hope that he may forgive you for having such a thought in your heart."*

4. **Acts 17:30** - *"Truly, these times of ignorance God overlooked, but now commands all men everywhere to repent."*

5. **1 Kings 8:46** - *"When they sin against you—for there is no one who does not sin—and you become angry with them and give them over to their enemies, who take them captive to their own lands, far away or near."*

6. **1 Chronicles 7:14** - *"If my people who are called by my name humble themselves, and pray and seek my face and turn from their wicked ways, then I will hear from heaven and will forgive their sin and heal their land."*

7. **1 John 1:8-9** - *"If we say we have no sin, we deceive ourselves, and the truth is not in us. If we confess our sins, he is faithful and just to forgive us our sins and to cleanse us from all unrighteousness."*

8. **2 Chronicles 7:14** - *"If my people who are called by my name humble themselves, and pray and seek my face and turn from their wicked ways, then I will hear from heaven and will forgive their sin and heal their land."*

9. **2 Corinthians 7:1** - *"Therefore, since we have these promises,*

dear friends, let us purify ourselves from everything that contaminates body and spirit, perfecting holiness out of reverence for God."

10. **2 Corinthians 7:10** - *"For godly grief produces a repentance that leads to salvation without regret, whereas worldly grief produces death."*

11. **2 Peter 2:9** - *"Then the Lord knows how to rescue the godly from trials, and to keep the unrighteous under punishment until the day of judgment."*

12. **2 Peter 3:9** - *"The Lord is not slow to fulfill his promise as some count slowness, but is patient toward you, not wishing that any should perish, but that all should reach repentance."*

13. **Ezekiel 14:6** - *"Therefore say to the Israelites, 'This is what the Sovereign Lord says: Repent! Turn from your idols and renounce all your detestable practices!'"*

14. **Ezekiel 18:21** - *"But if a wicked person turns away from all the sins they have committed and keeps all my decrees and does what is just and right, that person will surely live; they will not die."*

15. **Ezekiel 18:23** - *"Do I take any pleasure in the death of the wicked? declares the Sovereign Lord. Rather, am I not pleased when they turn from their ways and live?"*

16. **Ezekiel 33:11** - *"As I live, declares the Lord God, I have no pleasure in the death of the wicked, but that the wicked turn from his way and live; turn back, turn back from your evil ways, for why will you die, O house of Israel?"*

17. **Ezekiel 33:19** - *"But if wicked people turn from their wickedness and do what is just and right, they will live by doing so."*

18. **Ezekiel 36:25** - *"Then I will sprinkle clean water on you, and you will be clean; I will cleanse you from all your impurities and from all your idols."*

19. **Exodus 34:6** - *"The Lord, the Lord, a God merciful and gracious, slow to anger, and abounding in steadfast love and faithfulness."*

20. **Hosea 14:4** - *"I will heal their waywardness and love them freely, for my anger has turned away from them."*

21. **Isaiah 1:16** - *"Wash and make yourselves clean. Take your evil deeds out of my sight; stop doing wrong."*

22. **Isaiah 30:15** - *"For thus said the Lord God, the Holy One of Israel, 'In returning and rest you shall be saved; in quietness and in trust shall be your strength.'"*

23. **Isaiah 44:22** - *"I have blotted out your transgressions like a cloud and your sins like mist; return to me, for I have redeemed you."*

24. **Isaiah 55:6** - *"Seek the Lord while he may be found; call on him while he is near."*

25. **Isaiah 55:7** - *"Let the wicked forsake their ways and the unrighteous their thoughts. Let them turn to the Lord, and he will have mercy on them, and to our God, for he will freely pardon."*

26. **James 5:16** - *"Therefore, confess your sins to one another and pray for one another, that you may be healed. The prayer of a righteous person has great power as it is working."*

27. **Jeremiah 3:14** - *"Return, O faithless children, declares the Lord; for I am your master; I will take you, one from a city and two from a family, and I will bring you to Zion."*

28. **Jeremiah 31:34** - *"For I will forgive their iniquity, and I will remember their sin no more."*

29. **Joel 2:13** - *"And rend your hearts and not your garments. Return to the Lord your God, for he is gracious and merciful, slow to anger, and abounding in steadfast love; and he relents over disaster."*

30. **Joel 2:25** - *"So I will restore to you the years that the swarming locust has eaten, the crawling locust, the consuming locust, and the chewing locust, my great army which I sent among you."*

31. **John 15:7** - *"If you abide in me, and my words abide in you, ask whatever you wish, and it will be done for you."*

32. **Lamentations 3:40** - *"Let us test and examine our ways, and return to the Lord!"*

33. **Luke 5:32** - *"I have not come to call the righteous, but sinners to repentance."*

34. **Luke 13:3** - *"But unless you repent, you too will all perish."*

35. **Luke 13:5** - *"But I tell you, unless you repent, you will all likewise perish."*

36. **Luke 15:7** - *"I tell you, there will be more joy in heaven over one sinner who repents than over ninety-nine righteous persons who need no repentance."*

37. **Luke 18:13** - *"But the tax collector, standing far off, would not even lift up his eyes to heaven, but beat his breast, saying, 'God, be merciful to me, a sinner!'"*

38. **Mark 1:15** - *"And saying, 'The time is fulfilled, and the kingdom of God is at hand; repent and believe in the gospel.'"*

39. **Matthew 3:1-2** - *"In those days John the Baptist came, preaching in the wilderness of Judea and saying, 'Repent, for the kingdom of heaven has come near.'"*

40. **Matthew 3:7** - *"But when he saw many of the Pharisees and Sadducees coming to his baptism, he said to them, 'You brood of vipers! Who warned you to flee from the wrath to come?'"*

41. **Matthew 4:17** - *"From that time on Jesus began to preach, 'Repent, for the kingdom of heaven has come near.'"*

42. **Matthew 6:6** - *"But when you pray, go into your room, close the door and pray to your Father, who is unseen. Then your Father, who sees what is done in secret, will reward you."*

43. **Matthew 9:13** - *"But go and learn what this means: 'I desire mercy, not sacrifice.' For I have not come to call the righteous, but sinners."*

44. **Micah 7:18** - *"Who is a God like you, who pardons sin and forgives the transgression of the remnant of his inheritance? You do not stay angry forever but delight to show mercy."*

45. **Psalm 32:5** - *"Then I acknowledged my sin to you and did not cover up my iniquity. I said, 'I will confess my transgressions to the Lord.' And you forgave the guilt of my sin."*

46. **Psalm 38:18** - *"I confess my iniquity; I am sorry for my sin."*

47. **Psalm 51:3** - *"For I know my transgressions, and my sin is always before me."*

48. **Psalm 51:10** - *"Create in me a clean heart, O God, and renew a right spirit within me."*

49. **Psalm 51:13** - *"Then I will teach transgressors your ways, so that sinners will turn back to you."*

50. **Psalm 51:17** - *"The sacrifices of God are a broken spirit; a broken and contrite heart, O God, you will not despise."*

51. **Psalm 103:8** - *"The Lord is merciful and gracious, slow to anger and abounding in steadfast love."*

52. **Psalm 145:8** - *"The Lord is gracious and compassionate, slow to anger and rich in love."*

53. **Revelation 3:19** - *"Those whom I love, I reprove and discipline, so be zealous and repent."*

54. **Romans 6:23** - *"For the wages of sin is death, but the gift of God is eternal life in Christ Jesus our Lord."*

55. **Proverbs 1:23** - *"Repent at my rebuke! Then I will pour out my thoughts to you, I will make known to you my teachings."*

56. **Proverbs 28:13** - *"Whoever conceals their sins does not prosper, but the one who confesses and renounces them finds mercy."*

57. **Revelation 3:19** - *"Those whom I love, I reprove and discipline, so be zealous and repent."*

9

QUOTES FOR FAITH

This is a chapter crafted to invigorate and fortify one's faith journey. Whether in moments of adversity, confusion, or seeking spiritual inspiration, the chapter acts as a guiding light. Through contemplation of these profound quotes, readers are urged to delve deeper into their faith, discovering renewal and strength in the eternal truths they hold.

1. **Joshua 1:9:** - *"Have I not commanded you? Be strong and courageous. Do not be frightened, and do not be dismayed, for the Lord your God is with you wherever you go."*

2. **Deuteronomy 20:4:** - *"For the Lord your God is the one who goes with you to fight for you against your enemies to give you victory."*

3. **Deuteronomy 31:6**: *"Be strong and courageous. Do not fear or be in dread of them, for it is the Lord your God who goes with you. He will not leave you or forsake you."*

4. **Exodus 14:14**: *"The Lord will fight for you; you need only to be still."*

5. **Joshua 1:9**: *"Have I not commanded you? Be strong and courageous. Do not be frightened, and do not be dismayed, for the Lord your God is with you wherever you go."*

6. **Proverbs 3:5**: *"Trust in the Lord with all your heart, and do not lean on your own understanding."*

7. **Proverbs 16:3**: *"Commit your work to the Lord, and your plans will be established."*

8. **Proverbs 18:10**: *"The name of the Lord is a strong tower; the righteous man runs into it and is safe."*

9. **Psalm 3:3**: *"But you, O Lord, are a shield about me, my glory, and the lifter of my head."*

10. **Psalm 4:8**: *"In peace, I will lie down and sleep, for you alone, Lord, make me dwell in safety."*

11. **Psalm 23:1**: *"The Lord is my shepherd; I shall not want."*

12. **Psalm 27:1**: *"The Lord is my light and my salvation; whom shall I fear? The Lord is the stronghold of my life; of whom shall I be afraid."*

13. **Psalm 28:7**: *"The Lord is my strength and my shield; in him my heart trusts, and I am helped; my heart exults, and with my song, I give thanks to him."*

14. **Psalm 32:8**: *"I will instruct you and teach you in the way you should go; I will counsel you with my eye upon you."*

15. **Psalm 34:4**: *"I sought the Lord, and he answered me and delivered me from all my fears."*

16. **Psalm 34:17**: *"The righteous cry out, and the Lord hears them; he delivers them from all their troubles."*

17. **Psalm 34:18**: *"The Lord is near to the brokenhearted and saves the crushed in spirit."*

18. **Psalm 37:4**: *"Delight yourself in the Lord, and he will give you the desires of your heart."*

19. **Psalm 37:23**: *"The steps of a man are established by the Lord when he delights in his way."*

20. **Psalm 145:14**: *"The Lord upholds all who are falling and raises up all who are bowed down."*

21. **Psalm 147:3**: *"He heals the brokenhearted and binds up their wounds."*

22. **Isaiah 40:29**: *"He gives power to the faint, and to him who has no might, he increases strength."*

23. **Isaiah 40:31**: *"But they who wait for the Lord shall renew their strength; they shall mount up with wings like eagles; they shall run and not be weary; they shall walk and not faint."*

24. **Isaiah 41:10**: *"Fear not, for I am with you; be not dismayed, for I am your God; I will strengthen you, I will help you, I will uphold you with my righteous right hand."*

25. **Isaiah 54:10**: *"For the mountains may depart and the hills be*

removed, but my steadfast love shall not depart from you, and my covenant of peace shall not be removed, says the Lord, who has compassion on you."

26. **Jeremiah 29:11**: "For I know the plans I have for you, declares the Lord, plans for welfare and not for evil, to give you a future and a hope."

27. **Matthew 6:33**: "But seek first the kingdom of God and his righteousness, and all these things will be added to you."

28. **Matthew 11:28**: "Come to me, all who labor and are heavy laden, and I will give you rest."

29. **Matthew 19:26**: "But Jesus looked at them and said, 'With man, this is impossible, but with God all things are possible.'"

30. **Matthew 26:41**: "Watch and pray that you may not enter into temptation. The spirit indeed is willing, but the flesh is weak."

31. **Matthew 28:20**: "Teaching them to observe all that I have commanded you. And behold, I am with you always, to the end of the age."

32. **Mark 11:24**: "Therefore I tell you, whatever you ask in prayer, believe that you have received it, and it will be yours."

33. **John 3:16**: "For God so loved the world, that he gave his only Son, that whoever believes in him should not perish but have eternal life."

34. **John 14:27**: "Peace I leave with you; my peace I give to you. Not as the world gives do I give to you. Let not your hearts be troubled, neither let them be afraid."

35. **John 15:5**: *"I am the vine; you are the branches. Whoever abides in me and I in him, he it is that bears much fruit, for apart from me you can do nothing."*

36. **Acts 18:10**: *"For I am with you, and no one is going to attack and harm you, because I have many people in this city."*

37. **Romans 5:8**: *"But God shows his love for us in that while we were still sinners, Christ died for us."*

38. **Romans 8:18**: *"For I consider that the sufferings of this present time are not worth comparing with the glory that is to be revealed to us."*

39. **Romans 8:28**: *"And we know that in all things God works for the good of those who love him, who have been called according to his purpose."*

40. **Romans 8:38-39**: *"For I am sure that neither death nor life, nor angels nor rulers, nor things present nor things to come, nor powers, nor height nor depth, nor anything else in all creation, will be able to separate us from the love of God in Christ Jesus our Lord."*

41. **Romans 12:2**: *"Do not be conformed to this world, but be transformed by the renewal of your mind, that by testing you may discern what is the will of God, what is good and acceptable and perfect."*

42. **Romans 15:13**: *"May the God of hope fill you with all joy and peace in believing, so that by the power of the Holy Spirit you may abound in hope."*

43. **1 Corinthians 13:4-7**: *"Love is patient and kind; love does not envy or boast; it is not arrogant or rude. It does not insist on its own way; it is not irritable or resentful; it does not rejoice at wrongdoing, but rejoices with the truth. Love bears all things, believes all things, hopes all things, endures all things."*

44. **1 Corinthians 15:58**: *"Therefore, my beloved brothers, be steadfast, immovable, always abounding in the work of the Lord, knowing that in the Lord your labor is not in vain."*

45. **2 Corinthians 5:7**: *"For we walk by faith, not by sight."*

46. **Galatians 2:20**: *"I have been crucified with Christ. It is no longer I who live, but Christ who lives in me. And the life I now live in the flesh I live by faith in the Son of God, who loved me and gave himself for me."*

47. **Galatians 5:22-23**: *"But the fruit of the Spirit is love, joy, peace, forbearance, kindness, goodness, faithfulness, gentleness, and self-control."*

48. **Ephesians 2:8-9**: *"For by grace you have been saved through faith. And this is not your own doing; it is the gift of God, not a result of works, so that no one may boast."*

49. **Ephesians 3:20**: *"Now to him who is able to do far more abundantly than all that we ask or think, according to the power at work within us."*

50. **Ephesians 6:10**: *"Finally, be strong in the Lord and in the strength of his might."*

51. **Philippians 4:6**: *"Do not be anxious about anything, but in everything by prayer and supplication with thanksgiving let your requests be made known to God."*

52. **Philippians 4:13**: *"I can do all things through him who strengthens me."*

53. **Philippians 4:19**: *"And my God will supply every need of yours according to his riches in glory in Christ Jesus.*

54. **Colossians 3:23**: *"Whatever you do, work heartily, as for the Lord and not for men."*

55. **1 Thessalonians 5:16-18**: *"Rejoice always, pray without ceasing, give thanks in all circumstances; for this is the will of God in Christ Jesus for you."*

56. **2 Thessalonians 3:3**: *"But the Lord is faithful. He will establish you and guard you against the evil one."*

57. **Hebrews 11:6**: *"And without faith, it is impossible to please him, for whoever would draw near to God must believe that he exists and that he rewards those who seek him."*

58. **Hebrews 12:2**: *"For the joy set before him, he endured the cross, scorning its shame, and sat down at the right hand of the throne of God."*

59. **James 1:6**: *"But let him ask in faith, with no doubting, for the one who doubts is like a wave of the sea that is driven and tossed by the wind."*

60. **1 John 4:16**: *"And we have known and believed the love that God has for us. God is love, and he who abides in love abides in God, and God in him."*

61. **1 John 5:14**: - *"And we are confident that he hears us whenever we ask for anything that pleases him."*

62. **Jude 1:24-25**: - *"Now to him who is able to keep you from stumbling and to present you blameless before the presence of his glory with great joy, to the only God, our Savior, through Jesus Christ our Lord, be glory, majesty, dominion, and authority, before all time and now and forever. Amen."*

63. **Revelation 21:4**: - *"He will wipe away every tear from their eyes, and death shall be no more, neither shall there be mourning, nor crying, nor pain anymore, for the former things have passed away."*

64. **Revelation 22:13**: - *"I am the Alpha and the Omega, the first and the last, the beginning and the end."*

10

QUOTES FOR STRENGTH

"Quotes for Strength" explores the profound wisdom found in the Bible, presenting a curated selection of verses aimed at inspiring and empowering readers through life's challenges. The chapter contains timeless passages offering solace, guidance, and resilience in times of adversity. These quotes range from tales of courage to promises of divine support, serving as beacons of hope and reminders of the unwavering strength attainable through faith and spiritual reflection. Whether confronting personal struggles or seeking guidance, "Quotes for Strength" provides comfort and inspiration derived from the enduring wisdom of the Scriptures.

1. **Psalm 23:1-3** - *"The Lord is my shepherd; I shall not want. He makes me lie down in green pastures. He leads me beside still waters. He restores my soul."*

2. **Psalm 23:4** - *"Even though I walk through the valley of the shadow of death, I will fear no evil, for you are with me; your rod and your staff, they comfort me."*

3. **Psalm 27:1** - *"The Lord is my light and my salvation; whom shall I fear? The Lord is the strength of my life; of whom shall I be afraid?"*

4. **Psalm 27:14** - *"Wait for the Lord; be strong, and let your heart take courage; wait for the Lord!"*

5. **Psalm 31:24** - *"Be strong, and let your heart take courage, all you who wait for the Lord!"*

6. **Psalm 34:4** - *"I sought the Lord, and he answered me and delivered me from all my fears."*

7. **Psalm 34:18** - *"The Lord is near to the brokenhearted and saves the crushed in spirit."*

8. **Psalm 46:1** - *"God is our refuge and strength, an ever-present help in trouble."*

9. **Psalm 55:22** - *"Cast your burden on the Lord, and he will sustain you; he will never permit the righteous to be moved."*

10. **Psalm 71:16** - *"I will go in the strength of the Lord God; I will make mention of your righteousness, of yours only."*

11. **Psalm 73:26** - *"My flesh and my heart may fail, but God is the strength of my heart and my portion forever."*

12. **Psalm 84:11** - *"For the Lord God is a sun and shield; the Lord bestows favor and honor. No good thing does he withhold from those who walk uprightly."*

13. **Psalm 91:4** - *"He will cover you with his pinions, and under his wings, you will find refuge; his faithfulness is a shield and buckler."*

14. **Psalm 118:6** - *"The Lord is on my side; I will not fear. What can man do to me?"*

15. **Psalm 118:14** - *"The Lord is my strength and my song; he has become my salvation."*

16. **Psalm 145:8** - *"The Lord is gracious and merciful, slow to anger and abounding in steadfast love."*

17. **Psalm 145:14** - *"The Lord upholds all who are falling and raises up all who are bowed down."*

18. **Psalm 145:18** - *"The Lord is near to all who call on him, to all who call on him in truth."*

19. **Proverbs 18:10** - *"The name of the Lord is a strong tower; the righteous run into it and are safe."*

20. **Isaiah 40:29** - *"He gives power to the faint, and to him who has no might he increases strength."*

21. **Isaiah 40:31** - *"But those who hope in the Lord will renew their strength. They will soar on wings like eagles; they will run and not grow weary, they will walk and not be faint."*

22. **Isaiah 41:10** - *"Fear not, for I am with you; be not dismayed, for I am your God; I will strengthen you, I will help you, I will uphold you with my righteous right hand."*

23. **Isaiah 41:13** - *"For I, the Lord your God, hold your right hand; it is I who say to you, 'Fear not, I am the one who helps you.'"*

24. **Nahum 1:7** - *"The Lord is good, a refuge in times of trouble. He cares for those who trust in him."*

25. **Zechariah 10:6** - *"I will strengthen the house of Judah, and I will save the house of Joseph. I will bring them back because I have compassion on them, and they shall be as though I had not rejected them, for I am the Lord their God and I will answer them."*

26. **Matthew 28:20** - *"And behold, I am with you always, to the end of the age."*

11

QUOTES FOR FAMILY

This chapter is dedicated to exploring the depth of familial bonds through sacred scriptures. It emphasizes the importance of love, unity, and responsibility within family dynamics. Through carefully chosen passages, readers are encouraged to reflect on biblical teachings to nurture resilient and spiritually enriched family connections. The chapter aims to guide readers towards harmonious and fulfilling familial relationships based on foundational principles drawn from the Bible.

1. **Deuteronomy 6:6-7**: *"And these words that I command you today shall be on your heart. You shall teach them diligently to your children, and shall talk of them when you sit in your house, and when you walk by the way, and when you lie down, and when you rise."*

2. **Exodus 20:12**: *"Honor your father and your mother, so that you may live long in the land the Lord your God is giving you."*

3. **Ephesians 6:4***: "Fathers, do not exasperate your children; instead, bring them up in the training and instruction of the Lord."*

4. **Proverbs 22:6***: "Start children off on the way they should go, and even when they are old, they will not turn from it."*

5. **Proverbs 10:1***: "A wise son brings joy to his father, but a foolish son brings grief to his mother."*

6. **Proverbs 17:6***: "Children's children are a crown to the aged, and parents are the pride of their children."*

7. **Joshua 24:15***: "But if serving the Lord seems undesirable to you, then choose for yourselves this day whom you will serve, whether the gods your ancestors served beyond the Euphrates, or the gods of the Amorites, in whose land you are living. But as for me and my household, we will serve the Lord."*

8. **Psalm 23:1***: "The Lord is my shepherd; I shall not want."*

9. **Acts 16:31***: "And they said, 'Believe in the Lord Jesus, and you will be saved, you and your household.'"*

10. **1 Corinthians 13:4***: "Love is patient, love is kind. It does not envy, it does not boast, it is not proud."*

11. **Galatians 5:22-23***: "But the fruit of the Spirit is love, joy, peace, forbearance, kindness, goodness, faithfulness, gentleness, and self-control. Against such things, there is no law."*

12. **Romans 13:1***: "Let every person be subject to the governing authorities. For there is no authority except from God, and those that exist have been instituted by God."*

13. **Proverbs 24:3**: *"A house is built by wisdom and becomes strong through good sense."*

14. **Psalm 86:11**: *"Train me, God, to walk straight; then I'll follow your true path."*

15. **Proverbs 17:17**: *"A friend loves at all times, and a brother is born for a time of adversity."*

16. **Proverbs 17:22**: *"A cheerful heart is good medicine, but a crushed spirit dries up the bones."*

17. **Proverbs 13:1**: *"A wise son heeds his father's instruction, but a mocker does not respond to rebukes."*

18. **Proverbs 12:4**: *"An excellent wife is the crown of her husband, but she who brings shame is like rottenness in his bones."*

19. **Proverbs 23:24**: *"The father of a righteous child has great joy; a man who fathers a wise son rejoices in him."*

20. **Psalm 27:1**: *"The Lord is my light and my salvation—whom shall I fear? The Lord is the stronghold of my life—of whom shall I be afraid."*

21. **Zephaniah 3:17**: *"The Lord your God is with you, the Mighty Warrior who saves. He will take great delight in you; in his love, he will no longer rebuke you, but will rejoice over you with singing."*

22. **Colossians 4:6**: *"Let your conversation be always full of grace, seasoned with salt, so that you may know how to answer everyone."*

23. **Romans 12:2**: *"Do not conform to the pattern of this world, but be transformed by the renewing of your mind. Then you will be able to test and approve what God's will is—his good, pleasing and perfect will."*

24. **Ephesians 4:29**: *"Do not let any unwholesome talk come out of your mouths, but only what is helpful for building others up according to their needs, that it may benefit those who listen."*

25. **Colossians 3:13**: *"Bear with each other and forgive one another if any of you has a grievance against someone. Forgive as the Lord forgave you."*

26. **James 1:19**: *"My dear brothers and sisters, take note of this: Everyone should be quick to listen, slow to speak and slow to become angry."*

27. **James 3:16**: *"For where you have envy and selfish ambition, there you find disorder and every evil practice."*

28. **Proverbs 15:1**: *"A gentle answer turns away wrath, but a harsh word stirs up anger."*

29. **Proverbs 16:24**: *"Pleasant words are a honeycomb, sweet to the soul and healing to the bones."*

30. **1 Corinthians 15:33**: *"Do not be misled: 'Bad company corrupts good character.'"*

31. **Proverbs 15:28**: *"The heart of the righteous weighs its answers, but the mouth of the wicked gushes evil."*

32. **Proverbs 18:22**: *"He who finds a wife finds what is good and receives favor from the Lord."*

33. **Colossians 3:18-19**: *"Wives, submit yourselves to your husbands, as is fitting in the Lord. Husbands, love your wives and do not be harsh with them."*

34. **Proverbs 6:20**: *"My son, keep your father's command and do not forsake your mother's teaching."*

35. **Proverbs 20:24**: *"A person's steps are directed by the Lord. How then can anyone understand their own way?"*

36. **Numbers 6:24-26**: *"The Lord bless you and keep you; the Lord make his face shine on you and be gracious to you; the Lord turn his face toward you and give you peace."*

37. **James 3:17**: *"But the wisdom that comes from heaven is first of all pure; then peace-loving, considerate, submissive, full of mercy and good fruit, impartial and sincere."*

38. **1 Samuel 16:7**: *"But the Lord said to Samuel, 'Do not consider his appearance or his height, for I have rejected him. The Lord does not look at the things people look at. People look at the outward appearance, but the Lord looks at the heart.'"*

39. **1 Timothy 5:8**: *"But if anyone does not provide for his relatives, and especially for members of his household, he has denied the faith and is worse than an unbeliever."*

40. **Philippians 2:3**: *"Do nothing out of selfish ambition or vain conceit. Rather, in humility value others above yourselves."*

41. **Psalm 127:3**: *"Behold, children are a heritage from the Lord, the fruit of the womb a reward."*

42. **Proverbs 13:2**: *"A man shall eat well by the fruit of his mouth, But the soul of the unfaithful feeds on violence."*

43. **Ephesians 5:25**: *"Husbands, love your wives, just as Christ loved the church and gave himself up for her."*

44. **Proverbs 31:30**: *"Charm is deceptive, and beauty is fleeting; but a woman who fears the Lord is to be praised."*

45. **2 Thessalonians 3:3**: *"But the Lord is faithful, and he will strengthen you and protect you from the evil one."*

12

QUOTES FOR GRIEF

"Quotes for Grief" provides solace and reflection through carefully chosen verses, guiding readers through times of loss with enduring hope from sacred texts. It serves as a compassionate companion, offering healing words to navigate personal loss and support others in their time of need, reminding of the strength within sacred scriptures.

1. **Psalm 3:3** *"But you, O Lord, are a shield about me, my glory, and the lifter of my head."*

2. **Psalm 9:9** *"The Lord is a stronghold for the oppressed, a stronghold in times of trouble."*

3. **Psalm 16:8** *"I have set the Lord always before me; because he is at my right hand, I shall not be shaken."*

4. **Psalm 23:1-4** *"The Lord is my shepherd; I shall not want. He makes me lie down in green pastures. He leads me beside*

still waters. He restores my soul. Even though I walk through the valley of the shadow of death, I will fear no evil, for you are with me; your rod and your staff, they comfort me."

5. **Psalm 27:1** *"The Lord is my light and my salvation; whom shall I fear? The Lord is the stronghold of my life; of whom shall I be afraid?"*

6. **Psalm 28:7** *"The Lord is my strength and my shield; in him my heart trusts, and I am helped; my heart exults, and with my song, I give thanks to him."*

7. **Psalm 34:17-18** *"The righteous cry out, and the Lord hears them; he delivers them from all their troubles. The Lord is near to the brokenhearted and saves the crushed in spirit."*

8. **Psalm 49:15** *"But God will ransom my soul from the power of Sheol, for he will receive me."*

9. **Psalm 55:22** *"Cast your burden on the Lord, and he will sustain you; he will never permit the righteous to be moved."*

10. **Psalm 73:26** *"My flesh and my heart may fail, but God is the strength of my heart and my portion forever."*

11. **Psalm 103:17** *"But the steadfast love of the Lord is from everlasting to everlasting on those who fear him, and his righteousness to children's children."*

12. **Psalm 116:15** *"Precious in the sight of the Lord is the death of his saints."*

13. **Psalm 145:14-18** *"The Lord upholds all who are falling and raises up all who are bowed down. The Lord is near to all who*

call on him, to all who call on him in truth. He fulfills the desire of those who fear him; he also hears their cry and saves them. The Lord preserves all who love him, but all the wicked he will destroy. My mouth will speak the praise of the Lord, and let all flesh bless his holy name forever and ever."

14. **Psalm 147:3** *"He heals the brokenhearted and binds up their wounds."*

15. **Isaiah 25:8** *"He will swallow up death forever; and the Lord God will wipe away tears from all faces."*

16. **Isaiah 40:31** *"But they who wait for the Lord shall renew their strength; they shall mount up with wings like eagles; they shall run and not be weary; they shall walk and not faint."*

17. **Isaiah 41:10** *"Fear not, for I am with you; be not dismayed, for I am your God; I will strengthen you, I will help you, I will uphold you with my righteous right hand."*

18. **Isaiah 57:1-2** *"The righteous man perishes, and no one lays it to heart; devout men are taken away while no one understands. For the righteous man is taken away from calamity; he enters into peace; they rest in their beds who walk in their uprightness."*

19. **Jeremiah 29:11** *"For I know the plans I have for you, declares the Lord, plans for welfare and not for evil, to give you a future and a hope."*

20. **Jeremiah 31:13** *"I will turn their mourning into joy; I will comfort them, and give them gladness for sorrow."*

21. **Matthew 5:4** *"Blessed are those who mourn, for they shall be comforted."*

22. **Matthew 11:28** *"Come to me, all who labor and are heavy laden, and I will give you rest."*

23. **Matthew 11:28** *"Come to me, all who labor and are heavy laden, and I will give you rest."*

24. **Matthew 5:4** *"Blessed are those who mourn, for they shall be comforted."*

25. **Matthew 5:4** *"Blessed are those who mourn, for they shall be comforted."*

26. **Matthew 5:4** *"Blessed are those who mourn, for they shall be comforted."*

27. **John 11:25-26** *"I am the resurrection and the life. Whoever believes in me, though he die, yet shall he live, and everyone who lives and believes in me shall never die. Do you believe this?"*

28. **John 14:27** *"Peace I leave with you; my peace I give to you. Not as the world gives do I give to you. Let not your hearts be troubled, neither let them be afraid."*

29. **John 16:33** *"I have said these things to you, that in me you may have peace. In the world, you will have tribulation. But take heart; I have overcome the world."*

30. **John 16:33** *"I have said these things to you, that in me you may have peace. In the world, you will have tribulation. But take heart; I have overcome the world."*

31. **Job 19:25** *"For I know that my Redeemer lives, and at the last he will stand upon the earth."*

32. **Nahum 1:7** *"The Lord is good, a stronghold in the day of trouble; he knows those who take refuge in him."*

33. **Philippians 4:7** *"And the peace of God, which surpasses all understanding, will guard your hearts and your minds in Christ Jesus."*

34. **Philippians 4:7** *"And the peace of God, which surpasses all understanding, will guard your hearts and your minds in Christ Jesus."*

35. **Philippians 4:7** *"And the peace of God, which surpasses all understanding, will guard your hearts and your minds in Christ Jesus."*

36. **Psalm 3:3** *"But you, O Lord, are a shield about me, my glory, and the lifter of my head."*

37. **Psalm 9:9** *"The Lord is a stronghold for the oppressed, a stronghold in times of trouble."*

38. **Psalm 16:8** *"I have set the Lord always before me; because he is at my right hand, I shall not be shaken."*

39. **Psalm 23:1-4** *"The Lord is my shepherd; I shall not want. He makes me lie down in green pastures. He leads me beside still waters. He restores my soul. Even though I walk through the valley of the shadow of death, I will fear no evil, for you are with me; your rod and your staff, they comfort me."*

40. **Psalm 27:1** *"The Lord is my light and my salvation; whom shall I fear? The Lord is the stronghold of my life; of whom shall I be afraid?"*

41. **Psalm 28:7** *"The Lord is my strength and my shield; in him my heart trusts, and I am helped; my heart exults, and with my song, I give thanks to him."*

42. **Psalm 34:17-18** *"The righteous cry out, and the Lord hears them; he delivers them from all their troubles. The Lord is near to the brokenhearted and saves the crushed in spirit."*

43. **Psalm 49:15** *"But God will ransom my soul from the power of Sheol, for he will receive me."*

44. **Psalm 55:22** *"Cast your burden on the Lord, and he will sustain you; he will never permit the righteous to be moved."*

45. **Psalm 73:26** *"My flesh and my heart may fail, but God is the strength of my heart and my portion forever."*

46. **Psalm 103:17** *"But the steadfast love of the Lord is from everlasting to everlasting on those who fear him, and his righteousness to children's children."*

47. **Psalm 116:15** *"Precious in the sight of the Lord is the death of his saints."*

48. **Psalm 145:14-18** *"The Lord upholds all who are falling and raises up all who are bowed down. The Lord is near to all who call on him, to all who call on him in truth. He fulfills the desire of those who fear him; he also hears their cry and saves them. The Lord preserves all who love him, but all the wicked he will*

destroy. My mouth will speak the praise of the Lord, and let all flesh bless his holy name forever and ever."

49. **Psalm 147:3** *"He heals the brokenhearted and binds up their wounds."*

50. **Isaiah 25:8** *"He will swallow up death forever; and the Lord God will wipe away tears from all faces."*

51. **Isaiah 40:31** *"But they who wait for the Lord shall renew their strength; they shall mount up with wings like eagles; they shall run and not be weary; they shall walk and not faint."*

52. **Isaiah 41:10** *"Fear not, for I am with you; be not dismayed, for I am your God; I will strengthen you, I will help you, I will uphold you with my righteous right hand."*

53. **Isaiah 57:1-2** *"The righteous man perishes, and no one lays it to heart; devout men are taken away while no one understands. For the righteous man is taken away from calamity; he enters into peace; they rest in their beds who walk in their uprightness."*

54. **Jeremiah 29:11** *"For I know the plans I have for you, declares the Lord, plans for welfare and not for evil, to give you a future and a hope."*

55. **Jeremiah 31:13** *"I will turn their mourning into joy; I will comfort them, and give them gladness for sorrow."*

56. **Matthew 5:4** *"Blessed are those who mourn, for they shall be comforted."*

57. **Matthew 11:28** *"Come to me, all who labor and are heavy laden, and I will give you rest."*

58. **Matthew 5:4** *"Blessed are those who mourn, for they shall be comforted."*

59. **Matthew 5:4** *"Blessed are those who mourn, for they shall be comforted."*

60. **Matthew 5:4** *"Blessed are those who mourn, for they shall be comforted."*

61. **John 11:25-26** *"I am the resurrection and the life. Whoever believes in me, though he die, yet shall he live, and everyone who lives and believes in me shall never die. Do you believe this?"*

62. **John 14:27** *"Peace I leave with you; my peace I give to you. Not as the world gives do I give to you. Let not your hearts be troubled, neither let them be afraid."*

63. **John 16:33** *"I have said these things to you, that in me you may have peace. In the world, you will have tribulation. But take heart; I have overcome the world."*

64. **John 16:33** *"I have said these things to you, that in me you may have peace. In the world, you will have tribulation. But take heart; I have overcome the world."*

65. **Job 19:25** *"For I know that my Redeemer lives, and at the last he will stand upon the earth."*

66. **Nahum 1:7** *"The Lord is good, a stronghold in the day of trouble; he knows those who take refuge in him."*

67. **Philippians 4:7** *"And the peace of God, which surpasses all understanding, will guard your hearts and your minds in Christ Jesus."*

13

QUOTES FOR ENCOURAGEMENT

This chapter offers timeless wisdom from the Bible, guiding readers through life's challenges with hope and resilience. Its uplifting verses inspire faith, strength in adversity, and comfort in distress, fostering belief in a brighter future. Whether facing personal trials or seeking solace, these biblical quotes provide steadfast encouragement, nurturing courage and perseverance on life's journey.

1. **Psalm 23:1** - *"The Lord is my shepherd; I shall not want."*

2. **Psalm 55:22** - *"Cast your burden on the Lord, and he will sustain you."*

3. **Joshua 1:9** - *"Be strong and courageous. Do not be afraid; do not be discouraged, for the Lord your God will be with you wherever you go."*

4. **Jeremiah 29:11** - *"For I know the plans I have for you, declares the Lord, plans for welfare and not for evil, to give you a future and a hope."*

5. **Proverbs 3:5** - *"Trust in the Lord with all your heart and lean not on your own understanding."*

6. **Matthew 11:28** - *"Come to me, all you who are weary and burdened, and I will give you rest."*

7. **Psalm 34:17** - *"The righteous cry out, and the Lord hears them; he delivers them from all their troubles."*

8. **Isaiah 41:10** - *"Fear not, for I am with you; be not dismayed, for I am your God; I will strengthen you, I will help you, I will uphold you with my righteous right hand."*

9. **Psalm 34:4** - *"I sought the Lord, and he answered me and delivered me from all my fears."*

10. **Psalm 34:18** - *"The Lord is near to the brokenhearted and saves the crushed in spirit."*

11. **John 14:27** - *"Peace I leave with you; my peace I give to you. Not as the world gives do I give to you. Let not your hearts be troubled, neither let them be afraid."*

12. **Isaiah 40:31** - *"But those who hope in the Lord will renew their strength. They will soar on wings like eagles; they will run and not grow weary, they will walk and not be faint."*

13. **Isaiah 43:2** - *"When you pass through the waters, I will be with you; and when you pass through the rivers, they will not sweep over you. When you walk through the fire, you will not be*

burned; the flames will not set you ablaze."

14. **Romans 8:28** - *"And we know that in all things God works for the good of those who love him, who have been called according to his purpose."*

15. **Psalm 9:9** - *"The Lord is a refuge for the oppressed, a stronghold in times of trouble."*

16. **Psalm 147:3** - *"He heals the brokenhearted and binds up their wounds."*

17. **Exodus 14:14** - *"The Lord will fight for you; you need only to be still."*

18. **Psalm 3:3** - *"But you, Lord, are a shield around me, my glory, the One who lifts my head high."*

19. **Psalm 121:1-2** - *"I lift up my eyes to the mountains—where does my help come from? My help comes from the Lord, the Maker of heaven and earth."*

20. **Psalm 145:14** - *"The Lord upholds all who fall and lifts up all who are bowed down."*

21. **Galatians 5:22-23** - *"But the fruit of the Spirit is love, joy, peace, forbearance, kindness, goodness, faithfulness, gentleness, and self-control. Against such things, there is no law."*

22. **Psalm 32:8** - *"I will instruct you and teach you in the way you should go; I will counsel you with my loving eye on you."*

23. **John 16:33** - *"I have said these things to you, that in me you may have peace. In the world, you will have tribulation. But take heart; I have overcome the world."*

24. **Nahum 1:7** - *"The Lord is good, a refuge in times of trouble. He cares for those who trust in him."*

25. **Psalm 27:1** - *"The Lord is my light and my salvation—whom shall I fear? The Lord is the stronghold of my life—of whom shall I be afraid?"*

26. **Psalm 37:23-24** - *"The steps of a man are established by the Lord, when he delights in his way; though he fall, he shall not be cast headlong, for the Lord upholds his hand."*

27. **Psalm 91:4** - *"He will cover you with his feathers, and under his wings, you will find refuge; his faithfulness will be your shield and rampart."*

28. **Psalm 40:1** - *"I waited patiently for the Lord; he inclined to me and heard my cry."*

29. **Romans 15:13** - *"May the God of hope fill you with all joy and peace as you trust in him, so that you may overflow with hope by the power of the Holy Spirit."*

30. **Zephaniah 3:17** - *"The Lord your God is with you, the Mighty Warrior who saves. He will take great delight in you; in his love, he will no longer rebuke you, but will rejoice over you with singing."*

31. **Proverbs 29:25** - *"The fear of man lays a snare, but whoever trusts in the Lord is safe."*

32. **James 1:12** - *"Blessed is the one who perseveres under trial because, having stood the test, that person will receive the crown of life that the Lord has promised to those who love him."*

33. **Psalm 86:15** - *"But you, O Lord, are a compassionate and gracious God, slow to anger, abounding in love and faithfulness."*

34. **Psalm 37:5** - *"Commit your way to the Lord; trust in him, and he will act."*

35. **Isaiah 40:29** - *"He gives strength to the weary and increases the power of the weak."*

36. **Matthew 11:28** - *"Come to me, all who labor and are heavy laden, and I will give you rest."*

37. **Psalm 91:2** - *"I will say of the Lord, 'He is my refuge and my fortress, my God, in whom I trust.'"*

38. **Psalm 145:8** - *"The Lord is gracious and merciful, slow to anger and abounding in steadfast love."*

39. **Galatians 6:7** - *"Do not be deceived: God is not mocked, for whatever one sows, that will he also reap."*

40. **Psalm 3:3** - *"But you, O Lord, are a shield about me, my glory, and the lifter of my head."*

41. **Job 23:10** - *"But he knows the way that I take; when he has tried me, I shall come out as gold."*

42. **Psalm 23:4** - *"Even though I walk through the valley of the shadow of death, I will fear no evil, for you are with me; your rod and your staff, they comfort me."*

43. **Philippians 4:13** - *"I can do all things through him who strengthens me."*

44. **Proverbs 3:7-8** - *"Be not wise in your own eyes; fear the Lord, and turn away from evil. It will be healing to your flesh and refreshment to your bones."*

45. **2 Corinthians 12:9** - *"But he said to me, 'My grace is sufficient for you, for my power is made perfect in weakness.'"*

46. **Psalm 91:1** - *"He who dwells in the shelter of the Most High will abide in the shadow of the Almighty."*

47. **Romans 8:18** - *"For I consider that the sufferings of this present time are not worth comparing with the glory that is to be revealed to us."*

48. **Psalm 145:18** - *"The Lord is near to all who call on him, to all who call on him in truth."*

49. **Nahum 1:7** - *"The Lord is good, a stronghold in the day of trouble; he knows those who take refuge in him."*

50. **Deuteronomy 31:6** - *"Be strong and courageous. Do not fear or be in dread of them, for it is the Lord your God who goes with you. He will not leave you or forsake you."*

14

QUOTES FOR DEPRESSION

"Quotes for Depression" explores poignant verses from sacred scriptures, offering guidance and comfort in despair. These quotes highlight enduring strength in faith, transformative hope, and divine love even in darkness. Amid the arduous journey of depression, biblical insights offer solace, courage, and purpose. They serve as beacons of hope, guiding towards healing and inner peace.

1. **Psalm 3:3** - *"But you, O Lord, are a shield about me, my glory, and the lifter of my head."*

2. **Psalm 9:9** - *"The Lord is a refuge for the oppressed, a stronghold in times of trouble."*

3. **Psalm 23:4** - *"Even though I walk through the darkest valley, I will fear no evil, for you are with me; your rod and your staff, they comfort me."*

4.   **Psalm 27:1** - *"The Lord is my light and my salvation; whom shall I fear? The Lord is the stronghold of my life; of whom shall I be afraid?"*

5.   **Psalm 28:7** - *"The Lord is my strength and my shield; in him my heart trusts, and I am helped; my heart exults, and with my song, I give thanks to him."*

6.   **Psalm 34:4** - *"I sought the Lord, and he answered me and delivered me from all my fears."*

7.   **Psalm 34:17** - *"The righteous cry out, and the Lord hears them; he delivers them from all their troubles."*

8.   **Psalm 34:18** - *"The Lord is near to the brokenhearted and saves the crushed in spirit."*

9.   **Psalm 42:11** - *"Why are you cast down, O my soul, and why are you in turmoil within me? Hope in God; for I shall again praise him, my salvation and my God."*

10. **Psalm 55:22** - *"Cast your burden on the Lord, and he will sustain you; he will never permit the righteous to be moved."*

11. **Psalm 145:14** - *"The Lord upholds all who are falling and raises up all who are bowed down."*

12. **Psalm 147:3** - *"He heals the brokenhearted and binds up their wounds."*

13. **Isaiah 40:31** - *"But they who wait for the Lord shall renew their strength; they shall mount up with wings like eagles; they shall run and not be weary; they shall walk and not faint."*

14. **Jeremiah 29:11** - *"For I know the plans I have for you, declares the Lord, plans for welfare and not for evil, to give you a future and a hope."*

15. **Matthew 11:28** - *"Come to me, all who labor and are heavy laden, and I will give you rest."*

16. **John 14:27** - *"Peace I leave with you; my peace I give to you. Not as the world gives do I give to you. Let not your hearts be troubled, neither let them be afraid."*

17. **John 16:33** - *"I have said these things to you, that in me you may have peace. In the world, you will have tribulation. But take heart; I have overcome the world."*

18. **Philippians 4:6-7** - *"Do not be anxious about anything, but in everything by prayer and supplication with thanksgiving let your requests be made known to God. And the peace of God, which surpasses all understanding, will guard your hearts and your minds in Christ Jesus."*

19. **Philippians 4:13** - *"I can do all things through him who strengthens me."*

20. **Revelation 21:4** - *"He will wipe away every tear from their eyes, and death shall be no more, neither shall there be mourning, nor crying, nor pain anymore, for the former things have passed away."*

15

QUOTES FOR SOBRIETY

Through carefully chosen verses from the Bible this chapter provides strength to those on the path of sobriety. Each quote acts as a beacon of hope, reminding individuals of their resilience and divine support. Whether facing temptation or struggle, these quotes illuminate the transformative power of faith and perseverance. They serve as reminders of the unwavering support on the journey to a sober life.

1. **Proverbs 17:22** - *"A joyful heart is good medicine, but a crushed spirit dries up the bones."*

2. **Philippians 4:6** - *"Do not be anxious about anything, but in everything by prayer and supplication with thanksgiving let your requests be made known to God."*

3. **Philippians 4:7** - *"And the peace of God, which surpasses all understanding, will guard your hearts and your minds in Christ Jesus."*

4. **Philippians 4:8** - *"Finally, brothers, whatever is true, whatever is honorable, whatever is just, whatever is pure, whatever is lovely, whatever is commendable, if there is any excellence, if there is anything worthy of praise, think about these things."*

5. **Philippians 4:13** - *"I can do all things through Christ who strengthens me."*

6. **1 Peter 5:8** - *"Be sober-minded; be watchful. Your adversary the devil prowls around like a roaring lion, seeking someone to devour."*

7. **2 Corinthians 5:17** - *"Therefore, if anyone is in Christ, he is a new creation. The old has passed away; behold, the new has come."*

8. **Ephesians 5:18** - *"And do not get drunk with wine, for that is debauchery, but be filled with the Spirit."*

9. **James 1:12** - *"Blessed is the man who remains steadfast under trial, for when he has stood the test, he will receive the crown of life, which God has promised to those who love him."*

10. **2 Timothy 1:7** - *"For God gave us a spirit not of fear but of power and love and self-control."*

11. **Galatians 5:16** - *"But I say, walk by the Spirit, and you will not gratify the desires of the flesh."*

12. **Matthew 26:41** - *"Watch and pray so that you will not fall into temptation. The spirit is willing, but the flesh is weak."*

13. **James 4:7** - *"Submit yourselves therefore to God. Resist the devil, and he will flee from you."*

14. **1 Corinthians 10:13** - *"No temptation has overtaken you that is not common to man. God is faithful, and he will not let you be tempted beyond your ability, but with the temptation, he will also provide the way of escape, that you may be able to endure it."*

15. **Psalm 27:1** - *"The Lord is my light and my salvation; whom shall I fear? The Lord is the stronghold of my life; of whom shall I be afraid."*

16. **Deuteronomy 31:6** - *"Be strong and courageous. Do not fear or be in dread of them, for it is the Lord your God who goes with you. He will not leave you or forsake you."*

17. **Psalm 34:4** - *"I sought the Lord, and he answered me and delivered me from all my fears."*

18. **Isaiah 58:11** - *"And the Lord will guide you continually and satisfy your desire in scorched places and make your bones strong; and you shall be like a watered garden, like a spring of water, whose waters do not fail."*

19. **Psalm 51:10** - *"Create in me a clean heart, O God, and renew a right spirit within me."*

20. **John 10:10** - *"The thief comes only to steal and kill and destroy. I came that they may have life and have it abundantly."*

21. **Jeremiah 29:11** - *"For I know the plans I have for you, declares the Lord, plans for welfare and not for evil, to give you a future and a hope."*

22. **Psalm 23:1** - *"The Lord is my shepherd; I shall not want."*

23. **1 Corinthians 9:27** - *"But I discipline my body and keep it under control, lest after preaching to others, I myself should be disqualified."*

24. **Titus 2:11-12** - *"For the grace of God has appeared, bringing salvation for all people, training us to renounce ungodliness and worldly passions, and to live self-controlled, upright, and godly lives in the present age."*

25. **Matthew 22:37** - *"And he said to him, 'You shall love the Lord your God with all your heart and with all your soul and with all your mind.'"*

26. **John 16:33** - *"I have said these things to you, that in me you may have peace. In the world, you will have tribulation. But take heart; I have overcome the world."*

27. **Galatians 5:22-23** - *"But the fruit of the Spirit is love, joy, peace, patience, kindness, goodness, faithfulness, gentleness, self-control; against such things, there is no law."*

28. **Galatians 6:9** - *"And let us not grow weary of doing good, for in due season we will reap, if we do not give up."*

29. **Psalm 31:14** - *"But I trust in you, O Lord; I say, 'You are my God.'"*

30. **Colossians 3:17** - *"And whatever you do, in word or deed, do everything in the name of the Lord Jesus, giving thanks to God the Father through him."*

31. **Psalm 37:23-24** - *"The steps of a man are established by the Lord, when he delights in his way; though he fall, he shall not be cast headlong, for the Lord upholds his hand."*

32. **Romans 12:2** - *"Do not be conformed to this world, but be transformed by the renewal of your mind, that by testing you may discern what is the will of God, what is good and acceptable and perfect."*

33. **Ephesians 4:30** - *"And do not grieve the Holy Spirit of God, by whom you were sealed for the day of redemption."*

34. **Psalm 3:3** - *"But you, O Lord, are a shield about me, my glory, and the lifter of my head."*

35. **Matthew 6:33** - *"But seek first the kingdom of God and his righteousness, and all these things will be added to you."*

36. **2 Timothy 4:7** - *"I have fought the good fight, I have finished the race, I have kept the faith."*

37. **2 Corinthians 10:4** - *"For the weapons of our warfare are not of the flesh but have divine power to destroy strongholds."*

38. **Revelation 21:4** - *"He will wipe away every tear from their eyes, and death shall be no more, neither shall there be mourning, nor crying, nor pain anymore, for the former things have passed away."*

39. **1 Timothy 1:16** - *"But I received mercy for this reason, that*

in me, as the foremost, Jesus Christ might display his perfect patience as an example to those who were to believe in him for eternal life."

40. **Proverbs 29:25** - *"The fear of man lays a snare, but whoever trusts in the Lord is safe."*

41. **Romans 8:38-39** - *"For I am sure that neither death nor life, nor angels nor rulers, nor things present nor things to come, nor powers, nor height nor depth, nor anything else in all creation, will be able to separate us from the love of God in Christ Jesus our Lord."*

42. **Proverbs 18:24** - *"A man of many companions may come to ruin, but there is a friend who sticks closer than a brother."*

43. **1 Samuel 16:7** - *"But the Lord said to Samuel, 'Do not look on his appearance or on the height of his stature, because I have rejected him. For the Lord sees not as man sees: man looks on the outward appearance, but the Lord looks on the heart.'"*

44. **Mark 10:52** - *"And Jesus said to him, 'Go your way; your faith has made you well.' And immediately he recovered his sight and followed him on the way."*

45. **2 Corinthians 4:17** - *"For the momentary lightness of our affliction is producing for us an eternal weight of glory beyond all measure."*

46. **John 14:1** - *"Let not your hearts be troubled. Believe in God; believe also in me."*

47. **Proverbs 15:13** - *"A glad heart makes a cheerful face, but by sorrow of heart the spirit is crushed."*

48. **2 Chronicles 7:14** - *"If my people who are called by my name humble themselves, and pray and seek my face and turn from their wicked ways, then I will hear from heaven and will forgive their sin and heal their land."*

49. **Isaiah 41:10** - *"Fear not, for I am with you; be not dismayed, for I am your God; I will strengthen you, I will help you, I will uphold you with my righteous right hand."*

16

QUOTES FOR
SPIRITUAL WARFARE

This is a pivotal chapter offering profound guidance amidst life's battles. It invites readers on a journey through scripture, presenting powerful quotations as armor for the soul during spiritual conflict. Drawing from timeless teachings, these quotes provide solace and inspiration to confront adversity with faith and resilience. Whether facing personal struggles or broader spiritual warfare, this chapter offers invaluable insights to navigate challenges with courage and conviction. It serves as a beacon of hope, guiding readers towards strength and spiritual fortitude.

1. **Ephesians 6:12** - *"For we do not wrestle against flesh and blood, but against the rulers, against the authorities, against the cosmic powers over this present darkness, against the spiritual forces of evil in the heavenly places."*

2. **2 Corinthians 10:3-4** - *"For though we walk in the flesh,*

we are not waging war according to the flesh. For the weapons of our warfare are not of the flesh but have divine power to destroy strongholds."

3. **James 4:7** - *"Submit yourselves therefore to God. Resist the devil, and he will flee from you."*

4. **1 Peter 5:8** - *"Be sober-minded; be watchful. Your adversary the devil prowls around like a roaring lion, seeking someone to devour."*

5. **Romans 12:21** - *"Do not be overcome by evil, but overcome evil with good."*

6. **2 Timothy 4:7** - *"I have fought the good fight, I have finished the race, I have kept the faith."*

7. **Psalm 144:1** - *"Blessed be the Lord, my rock, who trains my hands for war, and my fingers for battle."*

8. **Isaiah 54:17** - *"No weapon that is fashioned against you shall succeed, and you shall refute every tongue that rises against you in judgment. This is the heritage of the servants of the Lord and their vindication from me, declares the Lord."*

9. **1 John 4:4** - *"Little children, you are from God and have overcome them, for he who is in you is greater than he who is in the world."*

10. **Psalm 18:39** - *"For you equipped me with strength for the battle; you made those who rise against me sink under me."*

11. **2 Corinthians 2:11** - *"so that we would not be outwitted by Satan; for we are not ignorant of his designs."*

12. **Revelation 12:11** - *"And they have conquered him by the blood of the Lamb and by the word of their testimony, for they loved not their lives even unto death."*

13. **1 Corinthians 16:13** - *"Be watchful, stand firm in the faith, act like men, be strong."*

14. **1 Timothy 6:12** - *"Fight the good fight of the faith. Take hold of the eternal life to which you were called and about which you made the good confession in the presence of many witnesses."*

15. **Proverbs 21:31** - *"The horse is made ready for the day of battle, but the victory belongs to the Lord."*

16. **Psalm 91:1-2** - *"He who dwells in the secret place of the Most High shall abide under the shadow of the Almighty. I will say of the Lord, 'He is my refuge and my fortress; my God, in Him I will trust.'"*

17. **2 Thessalonians 3:3** - *"But the Lord is faithful. He will establish you and guard you against the evil one."*

18. **Ephesians 6:11** - *"Put on the whole armor of God, that you may be able to stand against the schemes of the devil."*

19. **2 Chronicles 20:15** - *"And he said, 'Listen, all Judah and inhabitants of Jerusalem and King Jehoshaphat: Thus says the Lord to you, 'Do not be afraid and do not be dismayed at this great horde, for the battle is not yours but God's.'"*

20. **Psalm 27:1** - *"The Lord is my light and my salvation; whom shall I fear? The Lord is the stronghold of my life; of whom shall I be afraid?"*

21. **Colossians 2:15** - *"He disarmed the rulers and authorities and put them to open shame, by triumphing over them in him."*

22. **1 Corinthians 15:57** - *"But thanks be to God, who gives us the victory through our Lord Jesus Christ."*

23. **Psalm 23:4** - *"Even though I walk through the valley of the shadow of death, I will fear no evil, for you are with me; your rod and your staff, they comfort me."*

24. **1 Peter 2:9** - *"But you are a chosen race, a royal priesthood, a holy nation, a people for his own possession, that you may proclaim the excellencies of him who called you out of darkness into his marvelous light."*

25. **1 John 5:4** - *"For everyone who has been born of God overcomes the world. And this is the victory that has overcome the world— our faith."*

26. **Psalm 34:17** - *"When the righteous cry for help, the Lord hears and delivers them out of all their troubles."*

27. **Isaiah 41:10** - *"Fear not, for I am with you; be not dismayed, for I am your God; I will strengthen you, I will help you, I will uphold you with my righteous right hand."*

28. **2 Corinthians 4:4** - *"In their case the god of this world has blinded the minds of the unbelievers, to keep them from seeing the light of the gospel of the glory of Christ, who is the image of God."*

29. **Psalm 144:2** - *"He is my steadfast love and my fortress, my stronghold and my deliverer, my shield and he in whom I take refuge, who subdues peoples under me."*

30. **Romans 8:37** - *"No, in all these things we are more than conquerors through him who loved us."*

31. **1 Corinthians 15:33** - *"Do not be deceived: 'Bad company ruins good morals.'"*

32. **Matthew 16:19** - *"I will give you the keys of the kingdom of heaven, and whatever you bind on earth shall be bound in heaven, and whatever you loose on earth shall be loosed in heaven."*

33. **Psalm 91:14-15** - *"Because he holds fast to me in love, I will deliver him; I will protect him, because he knows my name. When he calls to me, I will answer him; I will be with him in trouble; I will rescue him and honor him."*

34. **1 John 3:8** - *"Whoever makes a practice of sinning is of the devil, for the devil has been sinning from the beginning. The reason the Son of God appeared was to destroy the works of the devil."*

35. **Isaiah 59:19** - *"So they shall fear the name of the Lord from the west, and his glory from the rising of the sun; for he will come like a rushing stream, which the wind of the Lord drives."*

36. **Revelation 2:7** - *"He who has an ear, let him hear what the Spirit says to the churches. To the one who conquers, I will grant to eat of the tree of life, which is in the paradise of God."*

37. **2 Timothy 2:3-4** - *"Share in suffering as a good soldier of Christ Jesus. No soldier gets entangled in civilian pursuits, since his aim is to please the one who enlisted him."*

38. **Psalm 28:7** - *"The Lord is my strength and my shield; in him my heart trusts, and I am helped; my heart exults, and with my song, I give thanks to him."*

39. **1 John 5:18** - *"We know that everyone who has been born of God does not keep on sinning, but he who was born of God protects him, and the evil one does not touch him."*

40. **Romans 16:20** - *"The God of peace will soon crush Satan under your feet. The grace of our Lord Jesus Christ be with you."*

41. **1 Corinthians 10:13** - *"No temptation has overtaken you that is not common to man. God is faithful, and he will not let you be tempted beyond your ability, but with the temptation, he will also provide the way of escape, that you may be able to endure it."*

42. **Psalm 18:2** - *"The Lord is my rock and my fortress and my deliverer, my God, my rock, in whom I take refuge, my shield, and the horn of my salvation, my stronghold."*

43. **1 Thessalonians 5:8** - *"But since we belong to the day, let us be sober, having put on the breastplate of faith and love, and for a helmet, the hope of salvation."*

44. **Hebrews 4:12** - *"For the word of God is living and active, sharper than any two-edged sword, piercing to the division of soul and of spirit, of joints and of marrow, and discerning the thoughts and intentions of the heart."*

45. **Revelation 3:21** - *"The one who conquers, I will grant him to sit with me on my throne, as I also conquered and sat down with my Father on his throne."*

46. **Psalm 37:39** - *"The salvation of the righteous is from the Lord; he is their stronghold in the time of trouble."*

47. **1 Peter 1:5** - *"who by God's power are being guarded through faith for a salvation ready to be revealed in the last time."*

48. **Ephesians 1:21** - *"far above all rule and authority and power and dominion, and above every name that is named, not only in this age but also in the one to come."*

49. **Psalm 119:11** - *"I have stored up your word in my heart, that I might not sin against you."*

50. **1 Peter 4:1-2** - *"Since therefore Christ suffered in the flesh, arm yourselves with the same way of thinking, for whoever has suffered in the flesh has ceased from sin, so as to live for the rest of the time in the flesh no longer for human passions but for the will of God."*

51. **1 John 5:19** - *"We know that we are from God, and the whole world lies in the power of the evil one."*

52. **Romans 13:12** - *"The night is far gone; the day is at hand. So then let us cast off the works of darkness and put on the armor of light."*

53. **Revelation 21:7** - *"The one who conquers will have this heritage, and I will be his God and he will be my son."*

54. **Psalm 119:105** - *"Your word is a lamp to my feet and a light to my path."*

55. **1 Thessalonians 5:23** - *"Now may the God of peace himself sanctify you completely, and may your whole spirit and soul and body be kept blameless at the coming of our Lord Jesus Christ."*

56. **Revelation 17:14** - *"They will make war on the Lamb, and the Lamb will conquer them, for he is Lord of lords and King of kings, and those with him are called and chosen and faithful."*

57. **Psalm 51:10** - *"Create in me a clean heart, O God, and renew a right spirit within me."*

58. **1 Corinthians 15:25** - *"For he must reign until he has put all his enemies under his feet."*

59. **Psalm 119:165** - *"Great peace have those who love your law; nothing can make them stumble."*

60. **Revelation 12:9** - *"And the great dragon was thrown down, that ancient serpent, who is called the devil and Satan, the deceiver of the whole world—he was thrown down to the earth, and his angels were thrown down with him."*

61. **2 Thessalonians 3:2** - *"Pray that we may be delivered from wicked and evil people, for not everyone has faith."*

62. **Psalm 37:32-33** - *"The wicked watches for the righteous and seeks to put him to death. The Lord will not abandon him to his power or let him be condemned when he is brought to trial."*

63. **Romans 8:38-39** - *"For I am sure that neither death nor life, nor angels nor rulers, nor things present nor things to come, nor*

powers, nor height nor depth, nor anything else in all creation, will be able to separate us from the love of God in Christ Jesus our Lord."

64. **Revelation 19:11** - *"Then I saw heaven opened, and behold, a white horse! The one sitting on it is called Faithful and True, and in righteousness, he judges and makes war."*

65. **Psalm 55:22** - *"Cast your burden on the Lord, and he will sustain you; he will never permit the righteous to be moved."*

66. **Ephesians 3:20-21** - *"Now to him who is able to do far more abundantly than all that we ask or think, according to the power at work within us, to him be glory in the church and in Christ Jesus throughout all generations, forever and ever. Amen."*

67. **1 Peter 5:10** - *"And after you have suffered a little while, the God of all grace, who has called you to his eternal glory in Christ, will himself restore, confirm, strengthen, and establish you."*

68. **Psalm 46:1-2** - *"God is our refuge and strength, a very present help in trouble. Therefore, we will not fear though the earth gives way, though the mountains be moved into the heart of the sea."*

69. **Romans 8:31** - *"What then shall we say to these things? If God is for us, who can be against us?"*

70. **Revelation 22:12** - *"Behold, I am coming soon, bringing my recompense with me, to repay each one for what he has done."*

17

QUOTES FOR FORGIVENESS

The chapter 'Quotes for Forgiveness' explores the transformative power of forgiveness through timeless teachings. It invites readers on a journey of introspection and grace. Through reflections, it serves as a guiding light for those seeking solace and restoration, embracing the liberating path towards peace and redemption."

1. **Matthew 5:44-45**: *"But I say to you, Love your enemies and pray for those who persecute you, so that you may be sons of your Father who is in heaven. For he makes his sun rise on the evil and on the good, and sends rain on the just and on the unjust."*

2. **Matthew 6:12**: *"And forgive us our debts, as we also have forgiven our debtors."*

3. **Matthew 6:14**: *"For if you forgive others their trespasses, your heavenly Father will also forgive you."*

4. **Matthew 18:21-22**: *"Then Peter came to Jesus and asked, 'Lord, how many times shall I forgive my brother or sister who sins against me? Up to seven times?' Jesus answered, 'I tell you, not seven times, but seventy-seven times.'"*

5. **Mark 11:25**: *"And whenever you stand praying, forgive, if you have anything against anyone, so that your Father also who is in heaven may forgive you your trespasses."*

6. **Luke 6:27-28**: *"But I say to you who hear, Love your enemies, do good to those who hate you, bless those who curse you, pray for those who abuse you."*

7. **Luke 6:37**: *"Judge not, and you will not be judged; condemn not, and you will not be condemned; forgive, and you will be forgiven."*

8. **Luke 11:4**: *"And forgive us our sins, for we ourselves forgive everyone who is indebted to us. And lead us not into temptation."*

9. **Luke 17:3-4**: *"Pay attention to yourselves! If your brother sins, rebuke him, and if he repents, forgive him, and if he sins against you seven times in the day, and turns to you seven times, saying, 'I repent,' you must forgive him."*

10. **John 8:7**: *"And as they continued to ask him, he stood up and said to them, 'Let him who is without sin among you be the first to throw a stone at her.'"*

11. **Acts 3:19**: *"Repent, therefore, and turn again, that your sins may be blotted out."*

12. **Romans 12:20-21**: *"To the contrary, 'if your enemy is*

hungry, feed him; if he is thirsty, give him something to drink; for by so doing you will heap burning coals on his head.' Do not be overcome by evil, but overcome evil with good."

13. **Ephesians 4:31-32***: "Let all bitterness and wrath and anger and clamor and slander be put away from you, along with all malice. Be kind to one another, tenderhearted, forgiving one another, as God in Christ forgave you."*

14. **Colossians 3:13***: "Bearing with one another and, if one has a complaint against another, forgiving each other; as the Lord has forgiven you, so you also must forgive."*

15. **1 John 1:9***: "If we confess our sins, he is faithful and just to forgive us our sins and to cleanse us from all unrighteousness."*

18

QUOTES FOR BLESSINGS

"In Quotes for Blessings", readers are invited to explore the profound wisdom of the Bible, discovering blessings that offer solace, guidance, and gratitude in every circumstance. Through quotes, the chapter illuminates the transformative power of blessings, reminding us of divine grace in our lives. It serves as a beacon of hope, guiding us toward deeper appreciation of life's blessings and boundless love. Whether in adversity or triumph, these blessings weave moments of joy and hope into the fabric of our existence, enriching our journey through life's tapestry.

1. **Proverbs 10:22** - *"The blessing of the Lord makes rich, and he adds no sorrow with it."*

2. **Proverbs 3:13** - *"Blessed is the one who finds wisdom, and the one who gets understanding."*

3. **Psalm 1:1** - *"Blessed is the man who walks not in the counsel of the wicked, nor stands in the way of sinners, nor sits in the seat of scoffers."*

4. **Psalm 23:1** - *"The Lord is my shepherd; I shall not want."*

5. **Psalm 28:7** - *"The Lord is my strength and my shield; in him my heart trusts, and I am helped; my heart exults, and with my song I give thanks to him."*

6. **Psalm 29:11** - *"May the Lord bless you with peace!"*

7. **Psalm 33:12** - *"Blessed is the nation whose God is the Lord, the people whom he has chosen as his heritage!"*

8. **Psalm 41:1** - *"Blessed is the one who considers the poor! In the day of trouble, the Lord delivers him."*

9. **Psalm 68:19** - *"Blessed be the Lord, who daily bears us up; God is our salvation."*

10. **Psalm 90:17** - *"May the favor of the Lord our God be upon us, and establish the work of our hands upon us; yes, establish the work of our hands!"*

11. **Psalm 118:26** - *"Blessed is he who comes in the name of the Lord! We bless you from the house of the Lord."*

12. **Psalm 128:5** - *"The Lord bless you from Zion! May you see the prosperity of Jerusalem all the days of your life!"*

13. **Psalm 146:5** - *"Blessed is he whose help is the God of Jacob, whose hope is in the Lord his God."*

14. **Nahum 1:7** - *"The Lord is good, a stronghold in the day of trouble; he knows those who take refuge in him."*

15. **Jeremiah 17:7** - *"Blessed is the man who trusts in the Lord, whose trust is the Lord."*

16. **Matthew 5:3** - *"Blessed are the poor in spirit, for theirs is the kingdom of heaven."*

17. **Matthew 5:4** - *"Blessed are those who mourn, for they shall be comforted."*

18. **Matthew 5:5** - *"Blessed are the meek, for they shall inherit the earth."*

19. **Matthew 5:6** - *"Blessed are those who hunger and thirst for righteousness, for they shall be satisfied."*

20. **Matthew 5:7** - *"Blessed are the merciful, for they shall receive mercy."*

21. **Matthew 5:8** - *"Blessed are the pure in heart, for they shall see God."*

22. **Matthew 5:9** - *"Blessed are the peacemakers, for they shall be called sons of God."*

23. **Matthew 5:10** - *"Blessed are those who are persecuted for righteousness' sake, for theirs is the kingdom of heaven."*

24. **Romans 15:13** - *"May the God of hope fill you with all joy and peace in believing, so that by the power of the Holy Spirit you may abound in hope."*

25. **James 1:12** - *"Blessed is the man who remains steadfast under trial, for when he has stood the test, he will receive the crown of life, which God has promised to those who love him."*

26. **Genesis 49:25** - *"The Lord bless you with the blessings of the heavens above, the blessings of the deep that crouches beneath, blessings of the breasts and of the womb."*

27. **Numbers 6:24-25** - *"The Lord bless you and keep you; the Lord make his face to shine upon you and be gracious to you."*

28. **Ephesians 1:3** - *"Blessed be the God and Father of our Lord Jesus Christ, who has blessed us in Christ with every spiritual blessing in the heavenly places."*

19

QUOTES FOR SICKNESS AND END OF LIFE

This chapter offers solace and guidance through illness and the end of life. Drawing from the Bible's wisdom, it provides reassurance, hope, and strength for those facing these challenges. Carefully selected verses offer spiritual support, serving as a beacon of light in difficult times, offering comfort and encouragement throughout life's journey.

1. **Psalm 34:17** - *"The righteous cry out, and the Lord hears them; he delivers them from all their troubles."*

2. **Psalm 34:18** - *"The Lord is near to the brokenhearted and saves the crushed in spirit."*

3. **Psalm 41:3** - *"The Lord sustains them on their sickbed and restores them from their bed of illness."*

4. **Psalm 55:22** - *"Cast your burden on the Lord, and he will sustain you; he will never permit the righteous to be moved."*

5. **Psalm 73:26** - *"My flesh and my heart may fail, but God is the strength of my heart and my portion forever."*

6. **Psalm 103:2-3** - *"Bless the Lord, O my soul, and forget not all his benefits, who forgives all your iniquity, who heals all your diseases."*

7. **Psalm 118:17** - *"I will not die but live, and will proclaim what the Lord has done."*

8. **Psalm 121:7** - *"The Lord will keep you from all harm—he will watch over your life."*

9. **Psalm 147:3** - *"He heals the brokenhearted and binds up their wounds."*

10. **Isaiah 41:10** - *"Fear not, for I am with you; be not dismayed, for I am your God; I will strengthen you, I will help you, I will uphold you with my righteous right hand."*

11. **Isaiah 53:5** - *"But he was wounded for our transgressions; he was crushed for our iniquities; upon him was the chastisement that brought us peace, and with his stripes, we are healed."*

12. **Matthew 11:28** - *"Come to me, all who labor and are heavy laden, and I will give you rest."*

13. **John 14:27** - *"Peace I leave with you; my peace I give to you. Not as the world gives do I give to you. Let not your hearts be troubled, neither let them be afraid."*

14. **Romans 8:18** - *"For I consider that the sufferings of this present time are not worth comparing with the glory that is to be revealed to us."*

15. **Romans 8:28** - *"And we know that in all things God works for the good of those who love him, who have been called according to his purpose."*

16. **1 Peter 2:24** - *"He himself bore our sins in his body on the tree, that we might die to sin and live to righteousness. By his wounds, you have been healed."*

17. **1 Peter 5:10** - *"And after you have suffered a little while, the God of all grace, who has called you to his eternal glory in Christ, will himself restore, confirm, strengthen, and establish you."*

18. **Philippians 4:6-7** - *"Do not be anxious about anything, but in everything by prayer and supplication with thanksgiving let your requests be made known to God. And the peace of God, which surpasses all understanding, will guard your hearts and your minds in Christ Jesus."*

19. **2 Thessalonians 3:3** - *"But the Lord is faithful, and he will strengthen you and protect you from the evil one."*

20

QUOTES FOR DAILY PRAYERS

In this chapter, we have a selection of quotes specifically tailored to enrich your daily prayers, providing you with spiritual nourishment and guidance for every moment of your day. Whether seeking comfort, seeking guidance, or simply seeking to deepen your spiritual connection, these timeless words from scripture are here to accompany you on your journey of faith."

1. **Psalm 23:1** - *"The Lord is my shepherd; I shall not want."*

2. **Philippians 4:13** - *"I can do all things through Christ who strengthens me."*

3. **Psalm 145:18** - *"The Lord is near to all who call on him, to all who call on him in truth."*

4. **1 Peter 5:7** - *"Cast all your anxiety on him because he cares for you."*

5. **Jeremiah 29:11** - *"For I know the plans I have for you, declares the Lord, plans for welfare and not for evil, to give you a future and a hope."*

6. **Psalm 46:10** - *"Be still, and know that I am God."*

7. *Exodus 14:14* - *"The Lord will fight for you; you need only to be still."*

8. **Proverbs 3:5** - *"Trust in the Lord with all your heart and lean not on your own understanding."*

9. **Psalm 27:1** - *"The Lord is my light and my salvation; whom shall I fear? The Lord is the stronghold of my life; of whom shall I be afraid?"*

10. **Galatians 5:22-23** - *"But the fruit of the Spirit is love, joy, peace, forbearance, kindness, goodness, faithfulness, gentleness, and self-control."*

11. **Romans 8:28** - *"And we know that in all things God works for the good of those who love him, who have been called according to his purpose."*

12. **Psalm 37:4** - *"Delight yourself in the Lord, and he will give you the desires of your heart."*

13. **Psalm 145:8** - *"The Lord is gracious and compassionate, slow to anger and rich in love."*

14. **Psalm 51:10** - *"Create in me a clean heart, O God, and renew a right spirit within me."*

15. **Matthew 6:33** - *"But seek first his kingdom and his righteousness, and all these things will be given to you as well."*

16. **James 5:16** - *"The prayer of a righteous person is powerful and effective."*

17. **Philippians 4:6** - *"Do not be anxious about anything, but in every situation, by prayer and petition, with thanksgiving, present your requests to God."*

18. **Nahum 1:7** - *"The Lord is good, a refuge in times of trouble. He cares for those who trust in him."*

19. **Deuteronomy 31:6** - *"Be strong and courageous. Do not be afraid or terrified because of them, for the Lord your God goes with you; he will never leave you nor forsake you."*

20. **Proverbs 16:3** - *"Commit to the Lord whatever you do, and he will establish your plans."*

21

QUOTES FOR THANKSGIVING

"Quotes for Thanksgiving" is a chapter offering passages on gratitude. It encourages reflection on the Bible's wisdom, emphasizing the significance of thanksgiving. Serving as a beacon of hope, it reminds readers to express gratitude in all circumstances. Through these quotes, readers are urged to cultivate a thankful heart, fostering appreciation for life's blessings.

1. **1 Chronicles 16:34** - *"Give thanks to the Lord, for he is good; his love endures forever."*

2. **Psalm 9:1** - *"I will give thanks to you, Lord, with all my heart; I will tell of all your wonderful deeds."*

3. **Psalm 100:4** - *"Enter his gates with thanksgiving and his courts with praise; give thanks to him and praise his name."*

4. **Psalm 107:8** - *"Let them give thanks to the Lord for his unfailing love and his wonderful deeds for mankind."*

5. **Psalm 107:1** - *"Give thanks to the Lord, for he is good; his love endures forever."*

6. **Philippians 4:6** - *"Do not be anxious about anything, but in every situation, by prayer and petition, with thanksgiving, present your requests to God."*

7. **Psalm 69:30** - *"I will praise God's name in song and glorify him with thanksgiving."*

8. **Psalm 28:7** - *"The Lord is my strength and my shield; my heart trusts in him, and he helps me. My heart leaps for joy, and with my song I praise him."*

9. **Colossians 3:15** - *"Let the peace of Christ rule in your hearts, since as members of one body you were called to peace. And be thankful."*

10. **1 Thessalonians 5:16-18** - *"Rejoice always, pray continually, give thanks in all circumstances; for this is God's will for you in Christ Jesus."*

11. **Psalm 147:7** - *"Sing to the Lord with grateful praise; make music to our God on the harp."*

12. **Colossians 3:17** - *"And whatever you do, whether in word or deed, do it all in the name of the Lord Jesus, giving thanks to God the Father through him."*

13. **2 Corinthians 9:15** - *"Thanks be to God for his indescribable gift!"*

14. **Colossians 4:2** - *"Devote yourselves to prayer, being watchful and thankful."*

15. **Colossians 3:16** - *"Let the message of Christ dwell among you richly as you teach and admonish one another with all wisdom through psalms, hymns, and songs from the Spirit, singing to God with gratitude in your hearts."*

16. **Psalm 118:29** - *"Give thanks to the Lord, for he is good; his love endures forever."*

22

QUOTES FOR PROTECTION

This chapter explores wisdom from scripture on seeking protection amid life's challenges. Drawing from the Bible, we find guidance on using faith and divine intervention as shields against adversity. These passages offer solace and strength for both physical safety and spiritual fortitude. Join us in discovering the transformative power of biblical wisdom in safeguarding and nurturing our lives.

1. **Deuteronomy 31:6** - *"Be strong and courageous. Do not fear or be in dread of them, for it is the Lord your God who goes with you. He will not leave you or forsake you."*

2. **Exodus 14:14** - *"The Lord will fight for you, and you have only to be silent."*

3. **Isaiah 41:13** - *"For I, the Lord your God, hold your right hand; it is I who say to you, 'Fear not, I am the one who helps you.'"*

4. **Nahum 1:7** - *"The Lord is good, a stronghold in the day of trouble; he knows those who take refuge in him."*

5. **Proverbs 18:10** - *"The name of the Lord is a strong tower; the righteous run into it and are safe."*

6. **Psalm 3:3** - *"But you, O Lord, are a shield about me, my glory, and the lifter of my head."*

7. **Psalm 5:11** - *"But let all who take refuge in you rejoice; let them ever sing for joy, and spread your protection over them, that those who love your name may exult in you."*

8. **Psalm 9:9** - *"The Lord is a stronghold for the oppressed, a stronghold in times of trouble."*

9. **Psalm 18:2** - *"The Lord is my rock and my fortress and my deliverer, my God, my rock, in whom I take refuge, my shield, and the horn of my salvation, my stronghold."*

10. **Psalm 23:1** - *"The Lord is my shepherd; I shall not want."*

11. **Psalm 27:1** - *"The Lord is my light and my salvation; whom shall I fear? The Lord is the stronghold of my life; of whom shall I be afraid?"*

12. **Psalm 28:7** - *"The Lord is my strength and my shield; in him, my heart trusts, and I am helped; my heart exults, and with my song, I give thanks to him."*

13. **Psalm 32:7** - *"You are a hiding place for me; you preserve me from trouble; you surround me with shouts of deliverance."*

14. **Psalm 34:7** - *"The angel of the Lord encamps around those who fear him, and delivers them."*

15. **Psalm 46:1** - *"God is our refuge and strength, a very present help in trouble."*

16. **Psalm 84:11** - *"For the Lord God is a sun and shield; the Lord bestows favor and honor. No good thing does he withhold from those who walk uprightly."*

17. **Psalm 91:1** - *"He who dwells in the shelter of the Most High will abide in the shadow of the Almighty."*

18. **Psalm 91:2** - *"I will say to the Lord, 'My refuge and my fortress, my God, in whom I trust.'"*

19. **Psalm 91:4** - *"He will cover you with his pinions, and under his wings, you will find refuge; his faithfulness is a shield and buckler."*

20. **Psalm 118:6** - *"The Lord is on my side; I will not fear. What can man do to me?"*

21. **Psalm 119:114** - *"You are my hiding place and my shield; I hope in your word."*

22. **Psalm 121:3** - *"He will not let your foot be moved; he who keeps you will not slumber."*

23. **Psalm 121:5** - *"The Lord is your keeper; the Lord is your shade on your right hand."*

24. **Psalm 121:7** - *"The Lord will keep you from all evil; he will keep your life."*

25. **Psalm 145:8-9** - *"The Lord is gracious and merciful, slow to anger and abounding in steadfast love. The Lord is good to all, and his mercy is over all that he has made."*

26. **Psalm 145:18** - *"The Lord is near to all who call on him, to all who call on him in truth."*

27. **Psalm 145:20** - *"The Lord preserves all who love him, but all the wicked he will destroy."*

28. **Psalm 34:18** - *"The Lord is near to the brokenhearted and saves the crushed in spirit."*

29. **2 Thessalonians 3:3** - *"But the Lord is faithful. He will establish you and guard you against the evil one."*

23

QUOTES AGAINST
SEXUAL IMMORALITY

The Bible, a cornerstone for Christian morality, addresses sexual integrity extensively, condemning immorality and emphasizing purity. This theme is explored in the chapter "Quotes Against Sexual Immorality," presenting verses condemning adultery and promoting fidelity in marriage. Readers are encouraged to reflect on these principles, recognizing their significance for personal fulfillment and communal well-being. Through clarity and conviction, the Scriptures offer timeless guidance on navigating the complexities of human sexuality, advocating for respect, commitment, and the sanctity of marriage. Upholding these values not only honors God but also fosters spiritual flourishing and societal harmony.

1. **1 Corinthians 6:18-20** - *"Flee from sexual immorality. All other sins a person commits are outside the body, but whoever sins*

sexually, sins against their own body. Do you not know that your bodies are temples of the Holy Spirit, who is in you, whom you have received from God? You are not your own; you were bought at a price. Therefore honor God with your bodies."

2. **Hebrews 13:4** - *"Marriage should be honored by all, and the marriage bed kept pure, for God will judge the adulterer and all the sexually immoral."*

3. **1 Thessalonians 4:3-5** - *"It is God's will that you should be sanctified: that you should avoid sexual immorality; that each of you should learn to control your own body in a way that is holy and honorable, not in passionate lust like the pagans, who do not know God."*

4. **Ephesians 5:3** - *"But among you there must not be even a hint of sexual immorality, or of any kind of impurity, or of greed, because these are improper for God's holy people."*

5. **Matthew 5:28** - *"But I tell you that anyone who looks at a woman lustfully has already committed adultery with her in his heart."*

6. **1 Corinthians 7:2** - *"But since sexual immorality is occurring, each man should have sexual relations with his own wife, and each woman with her own husband."*

7. **Colossians 3:5** - *"Put to death, therefore, whatever belongs to your earthly nature: sexual immorality, impurity, lust, evil desires and greed, which is idolatry."*

8. **Galatians 5:19-21** - *"The acts of the flesh are obvious: sexual immorality, impurity and debauchery; idolatry and witchcraft;*

hatred, discord, jealousy, fits of rage, selfish ambition, dissensions, factions and envy; drunkenness, orgies, and the like. I warn you, as I did before, that those who live like this will not inherit the kingdom of God."

9. **Proverbs 6:32** - *"But a man who commits adultery has no sense; whoever does so destroys himself."*

10. **1 Peter 2:11** - *"Dear friends, I urge you, as foreigners and exiles, to abstain from sinful desires, which wage war against your soul."*

11. **1 Corinthians 10:8** - *"We should not commit sexual immorality, as some of them did—and in one day twenty-three thousand of them died."*

12. **2 Timothy 2:22** - *"Flee the evil desires of youth and pursue righteousness, faith, love and peace, along with those who call on the Lord out of a pure heart."*

13. **Romans 13:13-14** - *"Let us behave decently, as in the daytime, not in carousing and drunkenness, not in sexual immorality and debauchery, not in dissension and jealousy. Rather, clothe yourselves with the Lord Jesus Christ, and do not think about how to gratify the desires of the flesh."*

14. **1 Corinthians 6:9-10** - *"Or do you not know that wrongdoers will not inherit the kingdom of God? Do not be deceived: Neither the sexually immoral nor idolaters nor adulterers nor men who have sex with men nor thieves nor the greedy nor drunkards nor slanderers nor swindlers will inherit the kingdom of God."*

15. **Ephesians 5:5** - *"For of this you can be sure: No immoral, impure or greedy person—such a person is an idolater—has any inheritance in the kingdom of Christ and of God."*

16. **1 Thessalonians 4:7** - *"For God did not call us to be impure, but to live a holy life."*

17. **Jude 1:7** - *"In a similar way, Sodom and Gomorrah and the surrounding towns gave themselves up to sexual immorality and perversion. They serve as an example of those who suffer the punishment of eternal fire."*

18. **Mark 7:21-23** - *"For it is from within, out of a person's heart, that evil thoughts come—sexual immorality, theft, murder, adultery, greed, malice, deceit, lewdness, envy, slander, arrogance and folly. All these evils come from inside and defile a person."*

19. **1 Corinthians 5:9-11** - *"I wrote to you in my letter not to associate with sexually immoral people—not at all meaning the people of this world who are immoral, or the greedy and swindlers, or idolaters. In that case, you would have to leave this world. But now I am writing to you that you must not associate with anyone who claims to be a brother or sister but is sexually immoral or greedy, an idolater or slanderer, a drunkard or swindler. Do not even eat with such people."*

20. **Revelation 21:8** - *"But the cowardly, the unbelieving, the vile, the murderers, the sexually immoral, those who practice magic arts, the idolaters and all liars—they will be consigned to the fiery lake of burning sulfur. This is the second death."*

21. **1 Corinthians 6:13** - *"You say, 'Food for the stomach and*

the stomach for food, and God will destroy them both.' The body, however, is not meant for sexual immorality but for the Lord, and the Lord for the body."

22. **1 Corinthians 6:15-16** - *"Do you not know that your bodies are members of Christ himself? Shall I then take the members of Christ and unite them with a prostitute? Never! Do you not know that he who unites himself with a prostitute is one with her in body? For it is said, 'The two will become one flesh.'"*

23. **1 Corinthians 6:19-20** - *"Do you not know that your bodies are temples of the Holy Spirit, who is in you, whom you have received from God? You are not your own; you were bought at a price. Therefore honor God with your bodies."*

24. **1 Corinthians 7:9** - *"But if they cannot control themselves, they should marry, for it is better to marry than to burn with passion."*

25. **Proverbs 5:3-4** - *"For the lips of the adulterous woman drip honey, and her speech is smoother than oil; but in the end, she is bitter as gall, sharp as a double-edged sword."*

26. **Proverbs 6:23-25** - *"For this command is a lamp, this teaching is a light, and correction and instruction are the way to life, keeping you from your neighbor's wife, from the smooth talk of a wayward woman. Do not lust in your heart after her beauty or let her captivate you with her eyes."*

27. **1 Thessalonians 4:4-5** - *"that each of you should learn to control your own body in a way that is holy and honorable, not in passionate lust like the pagans, who do not know God."*

28. **Colossians 3:2** - *"Set your minds on things above, not on earthly things."*

29. **Matthew 15:19** - *"For out of the heart come evil thoughts— murder, adultery, sexual immorality, theft, false testimony, slander."*

30. **1 Corinthians 15:33** - *"Do not be misled: 'Bad company corrupts good character.'"*

24

QUOTES AGAINST STEALING

"Quotes Against Stealing" presents timeless wisdom, urging readers to reflect on theft's moral implications. Drawing from biblical teachings, it illuminates integrity, honesty, and stewardship, guiding readers toward righteousness. Through profound verses and commentary, it highlights theft's harm to individuals and communities, advocating respect for others' possessions. This chapter prompts introspection, leading readers on a journey towards virtuous living grounded in scripture.

1. **Exodus 20:15** - *"You shall not steal."*

2. **Leviticus 19:11** - *"You shall not steal; you shall not deal falsely; you shall not lie to one another."*

3. **Matthew 19:18** - *"He said to him, 'Which ones?' And Jesus said, 'You shall not murder, You shall not commit adultery, You shall not steal, You shall not bear false witness.'"*

4. **Romans 13:9** - *"For the commandments, 'You shall not commit adultery, You shall not murder, You shall not steal, You shall not covet,' and any other commandment, are summed up in this word: 'You shall love your neighbor as yourself.'"*

5. **Ephesians 4:28** - *"Let the thief no longer steal, but rather let him labor, doing honest work with his own hands, so that he may have something to share with anyone in need."*

6. **Colossians 3:9** - *"Do not lie to one another, seeing that you have put off the old self with its practices."*

7. **1 Corinthians 6:10** - *"Nor thieves, nor the greedy, nor drunkards, nor revilers, nor swindlers will inherit the kingdom of God."*

8. **1 Peter 4:15** - *"But let none of you suffer as a murderer or a thief or an evildoer or as a meddler."*

9. **Proverbs 11:1** - *"A false balance is an abomination to the Lord, but a just weight is his delight."*

10. **Proverbs 16:8** - *"Better is a little with righteousness than great revenues with injustice."*

11. **Proverbs 20:17** - *"Bread gained by deceit is sweet to a man, but afterward his mouth will be full of gravel."*

12. **Zechariah 5:3** - *"Then he said to me, 'This is the curse that goes out over the face of the whole land. For everyone who steals*

shall be cleaned out according to what is on one side, and everyone who swears falsely shall be cleaned out according to what is on the other side.'"

13. **Luke 19:8** - *"And Zacchaeus stood and said to the Lord, 'Behold, Lord, the half of my goods I give to the poor. And if I have defrauded anyone of anything, I restore it fourfold.'"*

14. **1 Thessalonians 4:6** - *"That no one transgress and wrong his brother in this matter, because the Lord is an avenger in all these things, as we told you beforehand and solemnly warned you."*

15. **Deuteronomy 24:7** - *"If a man is found stealing one of his brothers of the people of Israel, and if he treats him as a slave or sells him, then that thief shall die. So you shall purge the evil from your midst."*

25

QUOTES FOR SETTING HEALTHY BOUNDARIES

"Quotes for Setting Healthy Boundaries" is a vital chapter offering insights from scripture on establishing healthy boundaries. Readers are guided to explore the importance of boundaries in relationships, responsibilities, and self-care through carefully selected quotes. This chapter empowers individuals to navigate life with grace and clarity, providing solace, strength, and practical advice rooted in biblical principles for a balanced and fulfilling life.

1. **Romans 12:2** - *"Do not be conformed to this world, but be transformed by the renewal of your mind."*

2. **Matthew 5:37** - *"Let your 'Yes' be 'Yes,' and your 'No,' 'No.'"*

3. **Philippians 4:13** - *"I can do all things through Christ who strengthens me."*

4. **2 Timothy 1:7** - *"For God gave us a spirit not of fear but of power and love and self-control."*

5. **Proverbs 4:23** - *"Above all else, guard your heart, for everything you do flows from it."*

6. **Colossians 3:2** - *"Set your minds on things that are above, not on things that are on earth."*

7. **Philippians 2:3** - *"Let nothing be done through selfish ambition or conceit, but in lowliness of mind let each esteem others better than himself."*

8. **Philippians 4:6** - *"Do not be anxious about anything, but in every situation, by prayer and petition, with thanksgiving, present your requests to God."*

9. **1 Corinthians 10:31** - *"So, whether you eat or drink, or whatever you do, do all to the glory of God."*

10. *Proverbs 29:25 - "The fear of man brings a snare, but whoever trusts in the Lord shall be safe."*

11. **Galatians 5:22-23** - *"But the fruit of the Spirit is love, joy, peace, forbearance, kindness, goodness, faithfulness, gentleness and self-control. Against such things there is no law."*

12. **1 Peter 5:8** - *"Be sober-minded; be watchful. Your adversary the devil prowls around like a roaring lion, seeking someone to devour."*

13. **Proverbs 29:11** - *"A fool gives full vent to his spirit, but a wise man quietly holds it back."*

14. **1 Corinthians 9:27** - *"But I discipline my body and keep it under control, lest after preaching to others I myself should be disqualified."*

15. **1 Corinthians 15:33** - *"Do not be deceived: 'Bad company ruins good morals.'"*

16. **Proverbs 15:1** - *"A soft answer turns away wrath, but a harsh word stirs up anger."*

17. **Psalm 23:1** - *"The Lord is my shepherd; I shall not want."*

18. **Psalm 16:8** - *"I have set the Lord always before me; because he is at my right hand, I shall not be shaken."*

19. **Galatians 5:1** - *"For freedom Christ has set us free; stand firm therefore, and do not submit again to a yoke of slavery."*

20. **2 Thessalonians 3:3** - *"But the Lord is faithful. He will establish you and guard you against the evil one."*

21. **Proverbs 16:32** - *"Whoever is slow to anger is better than the mighty, and he who rules his spirit than he who takes a city."*

22. **James 1:5** - *"If any of you lacks wisdom, let him ask God, who gives generously to all without reproach, and it will be given him."*

23. **Proverbs 22:3** - *"The prudent sees danger and hides himself, but the simple go on and suffer for it."*

24. **Hebrews 4:16** - *"Let us then with confidence draw near to the throne of grace, that we may receive mercy and find grace to help in time of need."*

25. **Galatians 6:7** - *"Do not be deceived: God is not mocked, for whatever one sows, that will he also reap."*

26. **James 1:12** - *"Blessed is the man who remains steadfast under trial, for when he has stood the test he will receive the crown of life, which God has promised to those who love him."*

27. **Romans 12:21** - *"Do not be overcome by evil, but overcome evil with good."*

28. **Philippians 4:7** - *"And the peace of God, which surpasses all understanding, will guard your hearts and your minds in Christ Jesus."*

29. **Romans 14:12** - *"So then each of us will give an account of himself to God."*

30. **Ephesians 6:11** - *"Put on the whole armor of God, that you may be able to stand against the schemes of the devil."*

31. **Psalm 34:18** - *"The Lord is near to the brokenhearted and saves the crushed in spirit."*

32. **1 Corinthians 14:33** - *"For God is not a God of confusion but of peace."*

33. **Proverbs 15:5** - *"A fool despises his father's instruction, but whoever heeds reproof is prudent."*

34. **Galatians 1:10** - *"For am I now seeking the approval of man, or of God? Or am I trying to please man? If I were still trying to please man, I would not be a servant of Christ."*

35. **Proverbs 16:9** - *"The heart of man plans his way, but the*

Lord establishes his steps."

36. **James 3:16** - *"For where jealousy and selfish ambition exist, there will be disorder and every vile practice."*

37. **James 3:17** - *"But the wisdom from above is first pure, then peaceable, gentle, open to reason, full of mercy and good fruits, impartial and sincere."*

38. **Proverbs 11:3** - *"The integrity of the upright guides them, but the crookedness of the treacherous destroys them."*

39. **1 Peter 3:9** - *"Do not repay evil for evil or reviling for reviling, but on the contrary, bless, for to this you were called, that you may obtain a blessing."*

40. **Proverbs 15:3** - *"The eyes of the Lord are in every place, keeping watch on the evil and the good."*

41. **Matthew 5:37** - *"But let your 'Yes' be 'Yes,' and your 'No,' 'No'; anything more than this comes from the evil one."*

42. **James 5:16** - *"Therefore, confess your sins to one another and pray for one another, that you may be healed."*

43. **Proverbs 14:26** - *"In the fear of the Lord one has strong confidence, and his children will have a refuge."*

44. **2 Timothy 2:22** - *"So flee youthful passions and pursue righteousness, faith, love, and peace, along with those who call on the Lord from a pure heart."*

45. **Proverbs 3:7** - *"Do not be wise in your own eyes; fear the Lord and turn away from evil."*

46. **Proverbs 15:18** - *"A hot-tempered man stirs up strife, but he who is slow to anger quiets contention."*

47. **2 Corinthians 6:14** - *"Do not be unequally yoked with unbelievers. For what partnership has righteousness with lawlessness?"*

48. **Ephesians 4:26** - *"Be angry and do not sin; do not let the sun go down on your anger."*

49. **Proverbs 25:28** - *"A man without self-control is like a city broken into and left without walls."*

50. **Galatians 6:9** - *"And let us not grow weary of doing good, for in due season we will reap, if we do not give up."*

51. **Psalm 5:11** - *"But let all who take refuge in you rejoice; let them ever sing for joy, and spread your protection over them, that those who love your name may exult in you."*

52. **Proverbs 18:6** - *"A fool's lips walk into a fight, and his mouth invites a beating."*

53. **Proverbs 18:24** - *"A man of many companions may come to ruin, but there is a friend who sticks closer than a brother."*

54. **Proverbs 3:27** - *"Do not withhold good from those to whom it is due, when it is in your power to do it."*

55. **James 1:19** - *"Know this, my beloved brothers: let every person be quick to hear, slow to speak, slow to anger."*

56. **James 1:26** - *"If anyone thinks he is religious and does not bridle his tongue but deceives his heart, this person's religion is worthless."*

57. **Proverbs 18:14** - *"A man's spirit will endure sickness, but a crushed spirit who can bear?"*

58. **Galatians 5:16** - *"But I say, walk by the Spirit, and you will not gratify the desires of the flesh."*

59. **Proverbs 18:16** - *"A man's gift makes room for him and brings him before the great."*

60. **Galatians 5:1** - *"For freedom Christ has set us free; stand firm therefore, and do not submit again to a yoke of slavery."*

61. **Romans 8:18** - *"For I consider that the sufferings of this present time are not worth comparing with the glory that is to be revealed to us."*

62. **Romans 8:28** - *"And we know that for those who love God all things work together for good, for those who are called according to his purpose."*

63. **2 Timothy 4:7** - *"I have fought the good fight, I have finished the race, I have kept the faith."*

64. **1 Corinthians 16:13** - *"Be watchful, stand firm in the faith, act like men, be strong."*

65. **Exodus 14:14** - *"The Lord will fight for you, and you have only to be silent."*

66. **Isaiah 26:3** - *"You will keep him in perfect peace whose mind is stayed on you because he trusts in you."*

67. **Deuteronomy 31:6** - *"Be strong and courageous. Do not fear or be in dread of them, for it is the Lord your God who goes with you. He will not leave you or forsake you."*

68. **Philippians 4:8** - *"Finally, brothers, whatever is true, whatever is honorable, whatever is just, whatever is pure, whatever is lovely, whatever is commendable, if there is any excellence, if there is anything worthy of praise, think about these things."*

69. **Matthew 6:33** - *"But seek first the kingdom of God and his righteousness, and all these things will be added to you."*

70. **Jeremiah 29:11** - *"For I know the plans I have for you, declares the Lord, plans for welfare and not for evil, to give you a future and a hope."*

71. **Psalm 37:23** - *"The steps of a man are established by the Lord, when he delights in his way."*

72. **Proverbs 3:6** - *"In all your ways acknowledge him, and he will make straight your paths."*

73. **Psalm 121:7** - *"The Lord will keep you from all evil; he will keep your life."*

74. **Philippians 4:19** - *"And my God will supply every need of yours according to his riches in glory in Christ Jesus."*

75. **Psalm 28:7** - *"The Lord is my strength and my shield; in him my heart trusts, and I am helped; my heart exults, and with my song, I give thanks to him."*

76. **Jeremiah 20:11** - *"But the Lord is with me like a mighty warrior; so my persecutors will stumble and not prevail."*

77. **John 16:33** - *"I have said these things to you, that in me you may have peace. In the world, you will have tribulation. But take heart; I have overcome the world."*

Conclusion

In closing this compilation of "Biblical Quotes for Life," we embark on a reflective journey through the various facets of human existence, illuminated by the timeless wisdom found in the Scriptures. The diverse range of topics covered in this book serves as a testament to the depth and breadth of guidance that the Bible offers for navigating the complexities of life.

The Scriptures have consistently emphasized the pursuit of knowledge and wisdom. As we conclude, let us carry with us the profound insights encapsulated in these quotes, recognizing the value of lifelong learning and the discernment that stems from a foundation rooted in divine wisdom.

The essence of love, as articulated in the Bible, permeates every aspect of our lives. May the quotes on love serve as a constant reminder of the transformative power of love, both in our relationship with the Creator and in our interactions with fellow human beings.

In the realm of commerce and finance, the Bible provides principles that guide ethical conduct and responsible stewardship. As we navigate the business world, may these quotes inspire integrity, fairness, and a commitment to the well-being of others.

The political arena is not exempt from the wisdom of the Scriptures. Let us carry with us the call to justice, righteousness, and servant leadership, as we engage in the complexities of governance and public service.

Family is the cornerstone of society, and the Bible offers invaluable guidance on marriage, parenting, and familial relationships. May these quotes foster strong, loving bonds within families and communities.

Acknowledging our imperfections is the first step towards spiritual growth. The quotes on sin, repentance, and faith remind us of the redemptive power of God's grace and the unwavering faith that sustains us through trials.

Life is filled with highs and lows, and the Scriptures offer solace and strength in times of distress. Let these quotes be a source of comfort, encouragement, and resilience in the face of adversity.

Battling personal demons and spiritual challenges is a universal human experience. The quotes on sobriety and spiritual warfare equip us with the spiritual armor needed to face such battles with courage and faith.

Forgiveness, blessings, and facing mortality are integral aspects of the human condition. May these quotes inspire a spirit of forgiveness, gratitude, and a deep understanding of the fragility of life.

The habit of daily prayer, thanksgiving, and seeking divine protection is a grounding force in our lives. Let these quotes serve as a foundation for a strong and resilient spiritual life.

Upholding moral standards is a shared responsibility. The quotes against sexual immorality and stealing underscore the importance of personal and societal ethics in fostering a just and compassionate world.

Establishing healthy boundaries is crucial for personal well-being and harmonious relationships. The Bible provides guidance on setting boundaries that align with love, respect, and self-care.

In concluding this journey through "Biblical Quotes for Life," may these timeless words continue to resonate in our hearts, guiding and inspiring us in our daily walk. May we find strength, wisdom, and grace in the pages of the Bible, applying its teachings to enrich our lives and the lives of those around us. As we close this chapter, let us carry the light of these quotes into the future, embracing the transformative power of faith, love, and divine wisdom.

About The Author

Dr. Robert Osobase has a Bachelor of Philosophy, Master of Social Work, and Doctoral degree in Healthcare Administration. He has worked in the healthcare industry since arriving the United States in 2007. Robert currently resides in Arlington, Texas.